DIARY OF AN ACCIDENTAL PSYCHIC

An ordinary man living an extraordinary life

Mark Bajerski

Dedicated with love to…
My Earth Angel, best friend and beautiful wife, Suzie.
Thank you for your endless trust in my passion. Your understanding, tolerance, strength, faith, and wisdom never cease to amaze me. Without you I would not be the man I am today and I could never have done this without you. I love you with all my heart.
And to my greatest teacher: my daughter, China.
Your love has shown me the way to being a more understanding and forgiving man. Thank you for your endless support and encouragement while Daddy put in many hours on this book and had to make some sacrifices. I love you, China. You are a truly beautiful soul.

ACKNOWLEDGEMENTS

Special thanks to Arlene Cashman for all your help in working with me on this book and even more so, for your beautiful friendship.

Thank you for your understanding of my ways, my life's work and my schedules! You gave me the strength to move forward, to believe in myself and you came with all the right energy to finally bring this book together. (Not to mention my expanded waistline from all the carrot cake that was consumed during the making of this book!) As you put it yourself, my words are the wool and you are the knitting needles! Bless you Arlene, and I truly hope our friendship lasts for one hundred lifetimes.

I would also like to thank Tricia Johnson for her amazing work and friendship. Not only for the final editing of my first book but also for her insights and enlightenment in understanding what I was trying to achieve with it.

To Andreas Holm, gifted photographer – thank you for such beautiful images, always inspirational.

Juan Antonio Garcia, film-maker – I'm so very grateful to you for always believing in me and for all the work you do, from the heart.

And to my two little furry friends – Daisy and Dennis (my loyal and much-loved Schnauzers!) who lead me on many paths of enlightenment!

CONTENTS

Spirit of Love and Healing

Spirit, thank you for gently guiding me and helping me along my path of Enlightenment; for those moments when I fell down and you lifted me back up; for the times you have protected me when I needed you the most.

Spirit, thank for the many tests you set out before me, for allowing me to see these tests and never pushing or influencing me.

Spirit, thank you for your love and guidance, through which I am a healthier, happier human being who enjoys living a balanced life.

Spirit, thank you for trusting in me; I am forever humbled by your presence and my respect towards you is of the greatest importance in my life now. You have helped me become the person I am today. You have allowed me to be the person that I wish to be; to shine that light for others.

Spirit, thank you for allowing me to see through your eyes, for bringing all the right people to my door and for believing in me.

Spirit, thank you for helping me to understand my purpose in this life, to help heal every single person around the world. I am no longer a man who spends his life 'chasing his tail.' I am a man who stands tall and still – like a lighthouse. What is needed of me is to be exactly where I am meant to be and to shine the light for others when in their darkest moments, just as you do for me.

Spirit, thank you, for now I know myself. I gratefully open my heart and allow your love to channel through me, spreading energy of purity, love and healing to my brothers and sisters, to the animals of this kingdom we share and to the beauty of nature we must protect in this world.

Mark Bajerski

Divine Intervention

You might wonder how I could call myself the 'Accidental Psychic' – thinking, of course, that I should always have known this 'vocation' was coming!

But if someone had said to me as a child that I would one day be a healer and tell people about their future, I would have thought they should have been on some kind of medication! No-one could have had a less 'spiritual' childhood than me, I believed, and I certainly had no inkling that my life would be so vastly different from all the other kids in my West Yorkshire town.

There were, in fact, many signs the Universe had laid out for me; signs that I somehow chose to not pay much attention to. But even if I had, how could I have understood what they had meant? At the age of twelve I'd lost my best friend – my beautiful mother - to cancer and was left with a father who was unable to show any love towards his children. My school life had been difficult due to my dyslexia – something quite unknown and not recognised when I was growing up. So often I was marched to the headmaster's office to take a punishment for being 'deliberately obstructive' in class. Had my teachers tried to understand my inner struggle - wanting so much to read like the others in my class and completely unable to do so - I am sure they might have behaved differently.

There had been quite a lot for me to struggle with during my early childhood years and yet, I was generally a happy child. Even back then, I took great delight in helping others. My mother was my best friend for more than a decade and she had taught me how to make the most of every situation. I grew up to be an ambitious and successful entrepreneur, married a most beautiful lady and became a father. But something was not quite right. I couldn't figure out what, but I knew my life was out of synch and the imbalance in it manifested itself through fears and physical pains. Although I was only a young man, I suffered years of ill health and, in particular, I had back problems and severe IBS (irritable bowel syndrome).

One day, after a spontaneous suggestion from my wife, my family and I started planning to leave our home in the UK to go and live in the Andalucian hills of southern Spain. This move was a family choice - we were seeking a new adventure. Somehow, the idea of living in Spain felt right for me too; I needed a change. Nothing about the move had been planned out meticulously and absolutely nothing could have prepared me for what was about to happen in my life. I genuinely believe that somehow, it was meant to be and now, seven years on, the ambitious and successful entrepreneur lives an entirely different life as an international psychic and healer.

Apart from working in my studio in Mijas, I am privileged to travel around the globe, working with so many people who have called for my help. In truth, I am a new man: one filled with love for life. I wake up each morning with so much happiness in my heart; I am free from years of health issues and I revel in the reality that life is amazing and can be pain-free. Through all I have experienced, I am left with no doubt that a higher intervention played the biggest part in where I find myself today and more precisely, in finding 'MYSELF!' I now understand that I am not alone, that I have *never* been alone in my struggles and that I was only ever a moment away from living a deeper, happier and more meaningful life. This is a constant cause of celebration to me, having spent decades just simply 'chasing my tail'.

Right now, YOU may be facing any number of struggles in your life. You may be seeking 'answers' or feel lost; unclear of your path or purpose. Even though you might enjoy many successes, there are times you might experience a curious sense of loss; emptiness... a wondering if there is really more to this life – YOUR life?

We spend so much of our energy worrying about careers, relationships and finances. It leads us down the rocky road to unrest, illness and, at the very least, many sleepless nights. Decision-making, and the 'what-if's' we line up before us often block us from change and moving forward. Time is a constant concern and our lives get tied up in past issues or frozen in fears about the future. We never seem to allow ourselves time to enjoy the moment.

We can become disconnected with the essence of 'life' and in doing so, when we lose a loved one, we can remain trapped too long in our grief; unable to lift ourselves up again. So often, we feel lost and very much alone. We become embittered about the pressures we feel we carry alone.

Whether you're religious or not, spiritual or not – ask yourself how often you have cried out to 'someone': *'Why? Why? Why?'* and felt devastated by the idea that no-one was listening? We lose faith in ourselves and feel completely disconnected from the idea that any higher power is here to help us. I know all these feelings and many more, as I once lived through them all.

The stories I am about to share with you in this diary carry a simple yet profound message of truth and it is this: you are not – and never will be – alone. All that is required of you as we journey together through the pages which follow is that you do so with an open heart and an open mind. Each story presents a true account of the point where divine intervention has taken place in a seemingly simple – yet profound – way in the lives of the many people I have had the pleasure to meet and read for.

As a psychic and healer, I witness first-hand how divine intervention - Spirit's 'helping hand'- instantly changes lives. People move beyond their fears; they move beyond pain – both physical and emotional. They move beyond the grief of losing loved ones to the spirit world.

What I hope to show you is that the universe is full of these higher, divine interventions - our signs and messages. You will learn how to heighten your awareness to recognise these signs and messages. Each unique story will provide an insight into the beauty and essence of HEALING, which is so very important in learning to live our lives 'in the moment.'

Once you reach this higher vibration and understanding about life, you may well find yourself asking '*Well, what now?*' Don't worry - this is why I have included a chapter on my own secrets and practices which will centre and focus you on what truly matters: who you really are!

Higher intervention takes us from the draining energies of fear, anxiety and pain and instills within us a vibrant energy of trust and belief, together with the knowledge that we are *NEVER ALONE.*

If you are going through a difficult and a painful time in your life, dealing with challenges, fears and uncertainty, then it might surprise you to know that this, in fact, is very good news indeed - because it is no coincidence that you are holding this book in your hand at this very moment. NOW is the moment of change!

"Whatever you are going through, and whatever you are feeling at this very moment, will one day fill your heart with so much love and understanding.
For what you are feeling right now will bring a new sense of awakening into your life: you will look back and realise how much you have grown."
- Mark Bajerski

THE HAND THAT SAVED ME

From my early childhood days, I'd had some level of awareness (signs) of the gifts and abilities granted to me. I had a sense of 'something' at work through a number of events that happened to me both as a child and into my early adult years. However, it was not until recent years that I achieved any real understanding of how I was to become a channel for their use. I would like to share one such event with you now.

It happened on a day much like any other. I was a typical eight-year-old boy making my way home after a game of football with my friends in the park. I remember enjoying the challenge of trying to bounce the ball all the way home in front of me while I'd replay the match over in my mind. On this particular day, I was so lost in my thoughts that I paid no attention to what was going on around me. Before I realised what was happening, I stepped out onto the road where a car was driving straight towards me. Gripped by fear, my body froze to the spot. All I could feel was my heart pounding in my chest; it seemed certain I was going to be hit. Miraculously, that was not to be the case. I felt the weight of a heavy hand grab my shoulder and pull my body backwards onto the curb. That hand saved my life.

I was completely stunned; my body was shaking and I was barely able to control my breathing. I just about managed to stammer out the words "Thank you!" as I turned to face the wonderful person who had saved me. To my total and utter amazement, there was no-one there. In fact, there was no-one anywhere near me at all. *But how could that be? I had definitely felt a hand. Someone had forcefully pulled me out of danger's way. Where were they now?*

I went home that day feeling most bewildered about what had occurred - but I was unable to talk to anyone about it. How could I? How could I explain any of it? And so this glorious event - this miracle - went untold until as recently as four years ago, when I sat with a lady who somehow knew I was 'different'. She asked if anything strange or peculiar had ever happened in my life - something that I was unable to explain. Even though I'd blocked it somewhat from my mind, the memory of that moment came rushing back. All the thoughts and feelings I'd experienced on that day returned as clearly and as sharply as if it had just happened yesterday. Only then, when I finally and openly shared the story of how my life had been spared that day, did I truly understand why this divine intervention had happened.

Throughout this book, I hope you will have the opportunity to learn more about the miracles brought about by divine intervention and draw your own conclusions about why Spirit spared me at that very moment.

"Finally, we allow ourselves to STOP and see all that has been given to us, in so many amazing ways.
We finally recognise the times when we have been protected.
We start to catch glimpses of the light; the light that is always shining about us, no matter what we are going through, or how long or how challenging our tests may be.
Take the time to just see: allow the gifts in your life to be revealed to you.
When that day arrives, your heart will smile with a new sense of life, and a new outlook on it.
You will know how truly amazing Spirit is.
We are the lucky ones and we should give thanks daily for being given the gift of each new day."

Mark Bajerski

Releasing the Spirit Within

Although I now recognise the many interventions I have experienced during my life, it was only as recently as seven years ago that I finally understood my life's purpose. And how *did* I start out on this amazing journey? When did I finally understand that I should lay down my auctioneer's hammer and continue on my journey here as a healer and psychic?

Well, this all began after our move to Spain and on a day when I'd had a chance encounter with a wonderfully smart lady. Incredibly elegant, she looked as if she had been born into royalty. Her striking white hair was perfectly groomed and she had a wonderfully warm smile. She spoke both directly and to the point. She explained how she used to be an estate agent and was now retired; that she had lived on the Costa del Sol for twenty-eight years and how she knew practically everyone. I guessed this was probably why she was making herself known to me, too – she wanted to find out who I was! All the same, I very much enjoyed our conversation at that first meeting, finding this lady both wise and interesting.

A week later, I received a call from her. She invited me along to her friend's house where she hoped I'd get to know some people. I was delighted to have the opportunity and happily accepted. When I arrived at a very nice house, I was immediately introduced everyone. There were around fifteen people present; men and women aged between fifty and eighty, all smartly dressed, gently-spoken and appearing very peaceful. They were very respect-ful towards me and towards each other. The house was large and very clean and I noted quite a collec-tion of beautiful artefacts of Buddha figures, angel pictures and Indian god statues. There were large pieces of stunning crystals displayed in all shapes and colours; music was playing softly in the back-ground and there was a strange smell of incense – a bit like at Sunday Mass, when the priest would swing the ball and the smell wafted around. I found the smell brought back certain memories of my childhood; memories which were kind of scary!

Finally, I noticed the dining table which was heavily laden with Danish cakes that looked mouth-wateringly amazing! This sight caused me to smile. Being a bit of a 'sweet tooth,' I couldn't wait to sink my teeth into them! The others were chatting amongst themselves in a language I didn't quite recognise – "Danish, my dear!'" my lady friend re-plied when I asked. With that, one of the gentlemen got up and turned down the music.

Everyone began to sit down quietly on chairs and sofas around the room and one by one, they closed their eyes. I wasn't quite sure what was going on. My friend turned, looked at me and smiled. "Sit down, close your eyes and relax, my dear," she said softly. I must admit I'd begun to feel somewhat uncomfortable and what happened next really threw me.

One sudden and synchronised sound filled the room. It appeared everyone present was literally humming out the strangest noise - "Ommmmm, Ommmm, Ommmm." Well, I'd never heard anything like this, having had no knowledge or experience of mantras or meditation at that point in my life. I was quite shaken by this strange turn of events. *'Oh, my Lord - help*!!' I thought, feeling very uneasy at this point; all kinds of notions were running through my head. It must be some type of cult, I decided; they were all completely mad! My mind was racing and I was ready to make a dash for the door. I worried that perhaps they may have locked it and if so, I'd probably look quite foolish trying to 'break out.' I was in a panic but said to myself, 'Hang in there, Mark." Thoughts of the table laden with cakes suddenly came into my mind and I thought at the very least, I'd have a chance to tuck into those Danish delights after this crazy night had ended.

My friend must have sensed my discomfort as she opened her eyes and quietly repeated, "Close your eyes, Mark, and relax." Seeing her warm smile, I felt a bit foolish to be so worried, so I did what I'd been told. With closed eyes, the time seemed to last forever but to my amazement, I did start to feel more relaxed - and even quite calm at one point. This was a strange feeling and a first for me - I am normally always on the go; the type of guy who goes on holiday and only manages to start unwinding by the last day!

Finally, after what seemed like an age, they all opened their eyes. The room was quiet and remained like that for another ten minutes or so. They talked quietly amongst themselves until finally, I got my reward and we all tucked into the gorgeous cakes. When I got home I talked to my wife, Suzie, explaining what I had just experienced. Describing my panic, Suzie burst out laughing. She laughed so much and actually, it was lovely to see this. She knows me so well, and she could imagine how stressful I would have found this entire situation.

Another week went by and my Danish friend called me up, once more inviting me back to their 'Danish Circle'. Ready for the call, I thanked her kindly and then quickly made my excuses why I couldn't make it. "Well," she said, "if you change your mind, I will wait for you at the roundabout down the hill at seven pm tonight."

I put the phone down and laughed.

"Who was it on the phone, Mark?" Suzie asked.

"My new Danish friend," I said, and smiled. "Imagine – she invited me back to the 'madhouse' again," I added, thinking Suzie would find that hilarious. However, she didn't find it funny at all – in fact, she was looking straight at me with a serious expression on her face. Then, to my amazement, she replied, "I think you should go."

"*What???*" I said. "I should *GO*? Are you nuts?"

"No, seriously, Mark," she said. "Since you went there last week you've really been a lot nicer to me, to be honest."

Hearing Suzie say that to me really stopped me in my tracks. Thinking about it, I realised that she was right; I had been a lot happier – not snapping back, not talking about negative things or feeling so sad.

I took a walk around the village that day, thinking over what Suzie had said to me. I realised that yes, I had been experiencing periods of real negativity – something I couldn't explain. Despite living in one of the most beautiful parts of the world, I felt an emptiness: a question mark about my life and its purpose. Something didn't feel 'right' and I was searching for an answer. In the end, I decided to return to the circle. For whatever reason, it had improved my mood for the better and made me a happier person. If it made my moods better and Suzie's life happier, then I would go again. I love Suzie dearly so it was well worth the sacrifice and, well, there were always those gorgeous cakes to look forward to!

So I went along and met up with my Danish friend that evening. As we travelled together to another friend's house, she explained exactly what these nights were all about. She told me the evenings are 'circles' and the main reason they all come together is to send healing thoughts to people who are not well. I thought that sounded fair enough - quite lovely actually - and I was much more relaxed as we drove up to the house. We received a warm greeting from those I had met the

DIARY OF AN ACCIDENTAL PSYCHIC

week before and they appeared quite excited to see me. A quick glance at the table with all the cakes on it made me feel uplifted; for those alone, tonight would be worth any sacrifice.

Just as it was on the first evening, we all sat with our eyes closed and the 'Ommmmm' began. Prepared this time, I was far more relaxed and as I closed my eyes, I found I felt quite a bit different - calmer and not so impatient for it to be over. As I got deeper into this moment of relaxation, I began to truly feel something; exactly what this feeling was, I had no real idea at the time. Today, I have come understand it and know it by its name: 'Energy'.

Once it had ended, my new friends began talking amongst themselves. Unable to speak to them in Danish, I had to sit quietly, all the while just longing to tuck into the tasty Danish cakes that seemed to accompany these evenings. I felt a bit like a schoolboy waiting for the bell to ring!

My thoughts were suddenly interrupted as my friend directed a question at me.

"Tell me Mark, what did *you* see?" she asked.

Everyone had stopped talking and seemed to be waiting for my reply.

"Sorry? What do you mean, what did I *see*? My eyes were closed all the time – I never opened them once," I explained truthfully.

She smiled and said, "No, Mark. When your eyes were *closed*, what did you see?"

A picture suddenly flashed into my mind. It came so quickly that I told myself to stop being silly; I would make a fool of myself.

"Um...nothing," I replied.

She looked at me more closely and said with real sincerity, "Mark, really, it doesn't matter. Whatever you saw, tell us about it. We won't laugh."

I was quite taken aback, thinking '*Wow! This lady can really read my mind!*'

"Think about it, Mark. What did you see?" she urged.

What followed then marked the start of my awakening - my true life path and my happiness. I closed my eyes; I felt quiet and relaxed. In one beautiful moment, I found my confidence. The picture returned. I described to the room how I'd seen a man's face: a man in his sixties with a white beard and white hair. He was laughing.

After I'd said this, I waited nervously for their reaction. They all looked at each other and smiled.

My friend turned to me. "Mark, tonight we were sending healing to a man who is very poorly at the moment," she explained. "Last week, with our healing thoughts, we began to help him get stronger. Today, his little granddaughter had blown bubbles in his face and for the first time in months, he laughed. This man is in his sixties, and has a white beard and white hair." The rush of feelings that overcame me could only be described as divine - a new journey had begun!

Conclusion

This is the story of the day when my divine life purpose was first revealed to me - a man with no understanding of the spiritual world. After the loss of my mother at the age of twelve, I was left with the belief that there is no God; how could there be? Yet all my life's lessons and journeys, with all the pains and sorrows, prepared me to become the perfect channel to do the work that I do. Right now, some of you may feel that a divine revelation such as this could never happen to you. But I believe Spirit finds a way to help us recognise 'WHO' we are, who we are meant to be and to show us our gifts. There is no discrimination with age and this divine moment may touch us at any time in our lives. I was a successful auctioneer one moment and the next, working with Spirit!

Each and every one of us has a higher divine life purpose, which can reveal itself in many ways. If you are yet to discover yours – and wouldn't it be magical if you discovered it through reading this book – promise me this: NEVER LOSE YOUR FAITH AND COURAGE. **BELIEVE IT - TO LIVE IT!**

Slowly I started to see my light.
I started to see that in this, my mirror, was a
beautiful person,
That all the fear I had was just an illusion and
it was my fear which was trying so hard to keep
me frozen.
Then, in my divine moment, I felt peace inside
me for the first time in my life.
I had finally made it; the lessons now all made
sense;
I finally let go and accepted me for who I was.
It was that easy, yet my mind made me believe I
could never do it....
But I did it !!!"
Mark Bajerski

Telepathy or Spirit?

I am often asked how I recognise Spirit coming through with messages, as opposed to me psychically tuning into someone's past, present and future - like a kind of telepathy. In truth, when I first began walking this path, it actually took me a while to believe entirely that it is in fact Spirit working through me. Now, a few years and many experiences later, I am left with absolutely no doubt whatsoever.

To give you an example, two sisters arrived one day at my psychic studio in Mijas Pueblo. They sat together for their readings and I began by explaining to them that although I never bring Spirit through, the door is always open. I began to tune into their past. I felt a doctor, who was part of the family, together with his two children and their characteristics. Then I tuned into another family member, who had sought help from a dishonest (male) solicitor. The information I received was to change to a lady solicitor. This all made sense to the women who were with me because they'd just found out their current solicitor was only interested in his fees and not the case itself. I also told

them information that helped to release painful issues in their current lives. Moving from one lady to
another, forty-five minutes passed in a flash.

What occurred next, however, was to be the
most significant part of their reading. I tuned into
their father and although it may sound incredible,
as I spoke, I could feel a burning sensation on my
back and head. Suddenly my ear 'popped' – much
like when you drive up a steep mountain – followed
by a gentle whistle. This is what regularly happens
to me now when Spirit channels through me.

I smiled and told the two ladies that their father was in the room. I knew they felt his presence
too and all three of us had tears in our eyes. I spoke
about how much he loved them and that he had
never left their side; about the many times they'd
played by a large oak tree and had picnics there.
The messages came through for about thirty minutes. I knew we'd gone way over the hour they'd
booked in for, but when this flow happens, time has
no importance and I carried on with their messages
of love and protection. I continued to speak about
his characteristics and what he felt for them both.
Then suddenly, as quickly as he had arrived, their
father's spirit was gone.

The two ladies had been listening intently to
my every word but for some reason, I could sense
some confusion. A silence followed and, a little concerned, I asked the ladies if anything had resonated
with them.

"Mark," one of the sisters replied. "Everything
you told us was incredibly accurate. That is, all except the things you said about our father."

I felt shocked to the core. *Why had Spirit given me all this information that now appeared to be incorrect?*

The lady continued, "Our mother fell pregnant within three months of marrying our father. She told us he left the very night she told him about her pregnancy and that he never once returned. We never got to know our father. So the information you gave us about him isn't correct." As this lady spoke, I felt Spirit come through again. Closing my eyes, I could see a picture of a man. He was wearing an army uniform and cap and he looked very happy. I noticed that he held a whip in his hand, like that used by horse riders.

My eyes opened and the words just came out, "You have a picture of your father in your pocket."

They both looked at me with shocked expressions. "Well yes," one replied. "We decided to bring along an old photo to show you. We thought you might be able to explain why he left before we were born. Our mother never really spoke of him and never told us the reason." They placed a photo on my table of a man in a dark suit standing next to a Victorian balloon-back chair. Then, I heard myself tell them something that would change their lives forever.

"This man...he is not your father," I said.

They turned to one another, completely baffled now.

"Mark, you must be mistaken. Are you *certain*? Our mother gave us this photo just before she died." They both looked quite torn and confused.

I looked directly at one of the sisters and heard myself say, "This is not the photo I wanted to see.

You have a photo of a man wearing an army uniform and a cap, with a horse whip in his hand?"

The question nearly threw her off her seat as she rummaged frantically in her bag to find her purse. Folded in one of the compartments was a photo. She placed it down on the table. Sure enough, this photo was as I'd seen in my vision. "Mark, this a photo of our *uncle* – what does this mean?" she said, looking very confused.

"This gentleman is in the room with us now and he tells me that this is the correct one," I said, pointing to the photo of the man in the army suit with the whip in his hand.

What followed was one of the most powerful divine interventions I have ever experienced. The father in Spirit had a message for these two ladies. It went something like this...

"My darling daughters, I was always in love with your mother. After the wedding of my brother to your mother, I'm afraid we made a terrible mistake that we kept secret from you both. When your mother found out she was pregnant, she told my brother about the affair. He took it very badly and left the very same night. He never came round; he never forgave us. I couldn't marry your mother for the shame it would have brought to the family, but I stayed close to look after you both. I wanted to tell you both every day, but the more time that passed, the harder it became. I wasn't sure you'd understand. I'm so very sorry, my dear, beautiful girls."

Revealing the truth about their father was incredibly emotional – but it was joyful too. As the ladies left my studio that day they felt so much lighter; it was as if all the pieces to a puzzle had been found for them. They explained cheerfully that indeed their uncle had lived close by and they had always considered him their father more than anyone. Everything made complete sense and although overcome by the news they'd received, they were very much at peace and ready to move forward with their happy lives.

Conclusion

We all possess what you may have often heard described as an 'aura.' Within our aura, there are fragments of our life that some people have the ability to tune into telepathically – and connect with them. But in this story, these ladies were not aware that their uncle was in fact their father, so I could not have received this information telepathically.

The only pure explanation for the truth being unveiled is one that requires faith and trust: quite simply, it was delivered by Spirit.

"Often, we walk a thousand miles in search of
the 'answers to life'.
Along our journey we look downwards, trying
to ensure our path remains safe.
So often, we lose sight of the very signs Spirit
intends for us.
Today make a new start!
Look UP and see the world in a different way;
in a new light.
Trust that your feet walk this path, your
journey protected at all times by the power of
Spirit.
In doing so, you will receive all your beautiful
answers, for you will have found your balance."
Mark Bajerski

Spirit's Guiding Light

I work mostly from my beautiful healing studio where I have an abundance of oils, crystals and other magical items which all contribute towards a wonderful experience for those who come to see me there. However, so often Spirit has a unique and special way to deliver a message. One such occasion occurred on a cold winter's day with a nice lady arriving at my studio for a reading.

I thought she might be feeling a bit chilly and so before we got started, I asked if she might like me to switch on another heater in the room.

"No thank you," she replied, "I'm fine. I've got a warm, heavy coat on."

She seemed happy enough and so I continued. We sat at opposite sides of my reading table, which has a spectacular, vibrant purple cloth over it and is laden with crystals, magical healing oils, figures of gods and angels and so much more. My eyes were fixed on an old set of cards I had not used for some time and I felt drawn to turning up the top card. I placed it on the table between us. On the card was an angel. The angel had a beautiful face, long, light-coloured hair and a big smile. Her arms were held

33

wide open. I tuned into the card to understand why I had been asked to select it, and also to reveal its message. A few moments went by and I continued to wonder. I wasn't picking up any feelings or signs at all from this card, so I kept asking 'Why?'

I looked for a moment through the skylark window above our heads. It was a very dark day outside and the sky was heavy with grey clouds. I felt myself smile at the beauty of the glass crystals which hang from this window.

Looking across again at the lady, I felt a kind of burning on the top of my head. Within seconds, a great light broke through the clouds and in through the skylark window. My heart warmed as I sensed Spirit 'working its magic.'

My eyes were drawn again towards the angel card where a most amazing thing had happened: a strong beam of sunlight which had entered the room was shining through one of my crystals and two small rays had fallen directly onto the card. I looked closely, realising that the sunrays were perfectly placed on the card, each ray resting on one of the angel's elbows. Asking Spirit for an explanation of this sign, I heard myself say, "Your elbows will get better and there is no need to worry."

Suddenly, tears were streaming down the lady's face. I could tell these were tears of joy and not pain or sorrow, and as we ended the reading, I asked if there was anything she would like to ask me which I had not mentioned.

'No thanks," was her reply, adding, "though I'd like to show you something." Excitedly, she began to remove the heavy coat she'd been wearing and she pulled up the sleeves of her jumper. Both her elbows had been cut deeply as if in an operation.

I smiled from ear to ear as she explained about two recent operations she'd had. Finding out that she would not need further surgery was music to her ears and one of the main reasons she had come for her reading that day. Remembering the card and how beautifully her question had been answered, all we could do was look up through the skylark window with a smile and say, "THANK YOU!"

Conclusion

Over the past years, I have been blessed to witness many such beautiful occasions where at just the right moment for a sign or an answer, there is nothing Spirit cannot do to make that happen. Each time I remember this moment, I am completely overwhelmed.

Spirit reveals the answers only when it is best for us - you cannot stop living your life, just waiting anxiously for such a moment. If you can believe that Spirit truly does bring forth messages, then you must also trust that you will receive one only when you really do need it most - not when you *think* you need it. As the saying goes, "A watched kettle never boils," and it is the same as if you put your life on hold, just waiting for a message or a sign. When you are in the presence of Spirit, you will see or feel the magic of how it works. The secret is to let your life flow, trusting that all will be given at the right *divine* moment.

"There are times in our lives when we are
tested.
These tests can bring FEAR into our lives: fear
of not knowing, of uncertainty and not being
able to see clearly.
There are moments when we feel trapped in
complete and utter darkness.
If and when you find yourself there, remember
that YOU can be the LIGHT....all you have to
do is ask, believe and trust.
Spirit always finds a way to help you - you are
never alone.
Be strong and know this, and you will be
shown the way."
It is within the darkness that we begin to see
the LIGHT more clearly; within the darkness,
Spirit is with you more than ever."
Mark Bajerski

TAKE A SPOONFUL OF SPIRIT

During psychic one-to-one readings and healings, I tune into what is often referred to as your 'aura' or 'life energy'. This divine gift is one which both humbles and amazes me, and it is one I respect with all my heart. As I tune in, there is no discrimination between the living and those who have passed. The feelings and connections to these fragments I tune into are equal. Protection from your family, friends and even your pets is always around you as they send out good energy and thoughts to you. Whether they are still living or have moved to the other side, their energy remains in our aura. I call these 'fragments of our being'. As I go deeper into the energy of protection within your aura, I 'feel' their thoughts and I receive very accurate information about each one of them, too. If they have passed to the other side, I simply deliver messages back to you reassuring you that they are around - helping, watching - and are happy. What I have learned is that most of all, they want YOU to be happy.

Should there ever be any ongoing issues, I do my best to try and resolve them there and then. Remember, each time you send out a thought to someone, it is a most powerful protection – so always make your thoughts loving and positive.

On one summer afternoon, I had a visit from a lovely lady who came for a future reading and pure energy healing. I could see she was a little nervous about any 'bad news' coming out from the reading. I spoke in kind, gentle words to reassure her that my work does not involve delivering 'bad' messages. I show those who ask for my help a number of different paths and help them to see any challenges or obstacles which may lie ahead on their journey. Information comes through to show how they may handle those challenges. It is not simply a matter of good or bad news – it is truly about receiving the messages which Spirit intends for you. And Spirit will always find ways to help us to see how we can conquer our challenges.

As I tuned into this lady's aura, I picked up her daughter's energy. I immediately felt there was a small issue which needed my attention. I spoke more about her lovely daughter and as I did so, I began to feel a sharp pain in the area of my stomach. Though the pain intensified, I continued as I knew I had to go deeper until I felt the pain ease; then I would know what needed to be said. As I finished the reading and healing, I asked this kind lady to do just one thing.

"Would you speak to your daughter about seeing her doctor for a check up?" I asked. She, of course, readily agreed. In a case like this, I always explain to my clients that I am *not* a doctor. In any case, it would certainly be better to go to a doctor and find out everything is fine, than not to go and later discover there was a small issue. I am strong enough to know that I could be wrong – I would never think I would always be right!

One week went by and a message appeared from this lady on my email. "Mark, you asked me to advise my daughter to have a check-up with her doctor and we just cannot thank you enough! The doctor found that her pancreas was not working correctly. If she had not gone when she did, it could have been very bad indeed.'

Another example happened when an Irish friend of mine, who had been coming to me for a while for healing, told me her story. An elderly Spanish man had begun to speak to her in a café on the Costa where she normally had her lunch. It was the first time she had ever talked to this man and he was just happy to share his memories of his time in Ireland in the fifties. She was enjoying hearing his impressions of Ireland when suddenly, he burst into a rendition of the popular Irish tune 'Galway Bay'. "*How funny!*" she thought – here was this wonderful Spanish man in his seventies, singing one of her father's favourite songs to her.

When she went back to work, she felt an immediate urge to speak to her father, who had been quite ill. As soon as he answered the phone, she knew something was wrong. Sure enough, he had fallen in his home just twenty minutes earlier - only able to reach for the telephone by pulling down on the cord. Had she not called at that moment, he could have been lying there for hours. She was able to act immediately to get help to him. She knew without a doubt that the song had been her message from

Spirit and that her father was being watched over and protected. Magic is always around. Stop for a moment in your busy life and listen, you never know - you just might feel something.

Conclusion

There are moments in life that can be seen as a kind of coincidence when, in reality, it is actually synchronicity (Spirit's helping hand) at work. Synchronicity happens around us every day, in magical signs and sparks. Perhaps you overhear a conversation which gives you an answer you needed to hear, or you glimpse a slogan on a poster as you drive down the road which resonates with you immediately. You may be out walking, with no real sense of where you are going, until you find yourself somewhere you needed to be in that exact moment in order to receive an answer. Always try to remain open to seeing your signs; they are all around us each and every day.

Walk out of your door, pick a flower and see what Mother Nature (Spirit) is telling you. She is always with us to help us along our paths. Have no doubt we are all loved: I knew that the lady's daughter was going to be fine because Spirit had guided her mother to my door.

"Listen to your heart, for this is our connection
to Spirit; our protection in this world.
Clear away the 'clutter' that you hold inside
your mind and become an empty vessel.
Allow yourself to be lovingly filled with
happiness.
In this happy state, you will receive so many
wonderful messages and gifts that will fill your
life with the strength to conquer anger, worry
and fear.
Within these messages, we are often gently
nudged in the right direction.
These divine moments happen each and every day.
Never doubt: this is Spirit's way of helping us."

Mark Bajerski

A Single Rose

Apart from the work I do in my healing studio, I very much enjoy participating in the healing fairs which are held around the world - and boy, do I meet some truly amazing people! At one such three-day psychic and healing fair in Malaga, I remember a tall lady approaching my stand and in a deep Spanish accent, asking for a reading. I began by placing my magical oil on her third eye. This oil is a particularly wonderful combination of more than two hundred essential oils and it contains literally hundreds of rare crystals. I spent more than two years in its making and I rub this oil on my hands each morning, receiving such a wonderful energy: it is a truly powerful healing oil and heart opener. As I asked the lady to put her left hand on my table, I reached over and held my right hand about three inches above hers. Closing my eyes, I went into what is known as 'alpha' mode. In this state, I experience a deep connection, with many feelings and sensations guiding me to the areas where healing is needed, or telling me what emotional issues exist.

I tuned into this kind lady's life and began to give her information that all made sense to her

- and even though her English was not perfect, she understood perfectly all that I shared with her. Then her mother, who is in the Spirit world, came through with a resounding presence. Over the years, I have come to know very clearly the difference between physically tuning into your aura and picking out fragments of your life, and Spirit actually coming through. In the latter case, my right ear literally 'pops,' followed by a high-pitched whistling sound. The hairs on my neck become sensitive and my head tingles. Spirit certainly likes to make an entrance!

She gave me a message to pass on to her daughter – a 'happy birthday' wish, as that day was indeed the day. She also sent a deep and genuine apology for not having been supportive and giving enough in life. The lady cried many tears but I could see happiness there, as it marked the beginning of 'letting go' from these past issues with her mother. She kissed me and left to go back to a stand at which she herself was working.

The next morning, I lay in bed drifting in and out of sleep. I was having a dream where I was given a bunch of flowers. I could see the flowers very clearly; they were all white except for one single red rose in the middle. Although the two ladies from the previous day were not present in my dream, I immediately felt a connection between the dream and the reading I had given them. I felt as if the mother was asking me to do something else; deliver another message. I took my beautiful daughter to school and then went to Mijas Pueblo gardens to meditate as I do every morning. I closed my eyes and again received a sudden vision of white flowers with a single red rose. It was almost as if someone was flashing a photo in my face, except this time, the image wouldn't go away. Thirty minutes later I decided to give up the meditation because this pushy mother's picture would not leave me. I walked my dogs, went for a coffee and then prepared to leave for the second day of the show. As I walked through the village, I enjoyed the hubbub of the Saturday market, where two lovely florists always have stalls in the small plaza. Then it happened. On this of all days, right in front of me was a display of white flowers with a bunch of red roses alongside! I laughed happily to myself and, without a second thought, asked for one white bunch with a single red rose in the middle. My heart stopped racing and a peaceful air of happiness came over me. One of the staff who works in my wife's shop happened to be at the market and began to praise me for being such a wonderful husband! '*Mmm...*' I thought to myself; this purchase was something I was going to have to explain to my wonderful wife later on - buying a bunch of flowers and then heading off to the Malaga fair to give them to another woman! Well that was a situation to sort out later in the day - at that moment, I was on a mission.

I arrived at the fair with my beautiful bunch of flowers in my hand. It suddenly occurred to me that I was going to walk up to someone who I hardly knew (apart from the fact that she had an extremely persistent mother in Spirit!) and give her a big bunch of flowers. I didn't have a clue how she might take that - and also, perhaps she had a boyfriend or husband with her on the stall? What would they say or do?

I waited nervously at her stand and caught a glimpse of her coming towards me. As she approached, I actually felt quite panicky, wondering what I would say – and hoping she wouldn't be angry or offended. She took a long look at me and then at the flowers in my hand. She said absolutely nothing and then, suddenly, burst into tears. I hurriedly tried to explain why I had done this but she raised up her hand to stop me; she knew exactly who had brought them and tearfully said; 'It's okay, I somehow knew this was going to happen.'

The fact that I had no need to explain myself felt extremely profound: it was clear this lady had understood the message – and to me, it felt magical.

Conclusion

There are times in our lives when we need to know our family on the other side are listening – and that they do care. Spirit works hard and lovingly every day to show us our signs, so you should always live with an open heart and mind. In doing so, you allow yourself to see and feel Spirit's light shining on you every single moment.

Spirit had already planned this day long before I met this lady.

And yes, I did explain to my wonderful wife what had happened, and she understood completely. To have such an understanding and caring support makes me who I am and I know that I am blessed to have found my soul mate and earth angel. Spirit looks out for us all.

"Even when they move into the light, the bond
we share with our loved ones never dies.
Our heart is the divine connection between our
two worlds, and all that is needed is for us to
slow down and listen with our hearts.
There are moments in our day when without
any conscious thought of our loved ones, they
are suddenly on our minds and in our hearts.
That is when Spirit is present.
When you feel this, STOP! Talk to your loved
ones; tell them you know they are with you.
Tell them how much you love them."

Mark Bajerski

Words of an Angel

I had been giving free angel card readings for about two years when on one typically sunny morning in Mijas, as I was opening up one of our two shops in the village, a lady walked slowly up the steps that led into the shop. As she approached, she looked at me, and said, "I honestly have no idea why I came to Mijas Pueblo today, other than I felt drawn to do so. I don't even know why I was walking up these steps but now that I've seen your sign on the wall, I wonder if you would give me an angel card reading?"

I smiled with an inner happiness, knowing that Spirit had led this lady to my door.

As we began her reading, I immediately felt a deep pain; one I now recognise as the tremendous pain of grief and loss. As my cards spoke, I picked up her wonderful husband in Spirit and I continued with all that needed to be said. We spoke about her life and marriage to this amazing man, and yet I couldn't help feeling that I had missed something. Even after we had hugged and said our goodbyes, I continued to mull things over, much as you do when trying to remember some niggling fact or detail you think you might have forgotten. These occasions are rare for me, though, and I felt a little upset.

As I walked around the shop, which was busy with new customers, something suddenly fell to the floor from a high shelf and landed right in front of my feet. I looked down in total amazement. It was one of our beautiful angel bookmarks. I know well enough not to question these occurrences – this was the missing message! Excited now, I knew I had to present the bookmark to the lady – but how? She had left a good ten minutes before and the chances of seeing her again were slim. Our village is flooded with tourists in the height of summer and I couldn't leave when it was full of customers. Agonising over what to do, I looked at the angel bookmark and read its message: *'My dear love, words couldn't say how I feel about you. You are my heart, my strength and my life. My love for you will never die and I give you an angel to watch over you and always keep you safe.'*

I closed my eyes as I needed to think how on earth I could find this lady. Suddenly, I received a strong and powerful vision and I could see her having a conversation with Suzie, my wife. With complete clarity, I took out my phone. Suzie, who was working in our other shop in the village, answered almost immediately and I told her, "Suzie, a lady has just had a reading with me and she will walk through your door within the next ten to fifteen minutes. You will know who she is when she comes. Can you please ask her to come back to see me, as I have another message for her."

Within minutes, the lady had arrived at the other shop. She walked straight up to Suzie, almost as if she were expecting a message. The two ladies were amazed and surprised because they both somehow felt a connection – but this, of course, was divine intervention at work. Having received the message from Suzie, she hurried back to speak to me at my studio. I was so relieved as I handed her the bookmark, and explained gently what had happened. Many tears were shed during those moments; tears of pure love and joy in the knowing that her husband was still so very near. For me, it was WOW. The final piece of the puzzle was in place and I now felt happy that my work was complete.

Conclusion

The universe is a magical place which pulls people in the direction of help. I trusted in my vision and had complete confidence that the lady would be drawn towards my wife. Suzie trusted that she would recognise this lady and have her return to meet me again. There are times we must **trust** in a power that is beyond our understanding.

Without question, this lady's late husband played the greatest part of all in this day – and the event registered deep within my soul. If you have lost someone close, take comfort and know that his or her energy is always around you.

"Often we find ourselves in a certain place and time, not really sure 'WHY?'
This is how divine intervention can play a part, allowing us to receive small yet powerful signs of reassurance that Spirit - our loved ones on the other side - are always with us, watching over us, healing us.
Have trust that we are truly blessed and we are all protected in more ways than one could ever imagine.
Learn not to question 'WHY?'
Instead, look up and say, 'Thank you, Spirit, for your intervention; I believe you did this for my higher good.'
Spirit's intervention is here to guide us on a path to a higher level of peace and happiness"

Mark Bajerski

THE ART OF TAROT

One of the things I appreciate most about living in my magical, mountain-top village is the way the locals still stop on the street to catch up with each other. Sadly, in bigger towns and cities, this neighbourly connection does not always exist. Thanks to this lovely sense of community, I found myself enjoying a coffee one particular morning with a most wonderful couple who lived very close to me at the time. We were talking about all the usual things: the nice pace of life, the sunshine etc, and then they asked if everything was going well in my life – if I was happy.

"Yes, very happy thank you," I replied.

Then the lady asked me almost apologetically, "Sorry Mark, but can you tell us exactly *what* it is you do for a living?"

I smiled as I replied, "Well, I *used* to run a shop in the village but now I am on a *very* different path.'

"Oooh, interesting," she replied, clearly intrigued. "Come on then; tell us what it is you're doing now!"

So I continued, "I work upstairs above my wife's shop. I have started giving healing and I also read angel cards. Actually, just recently, I have started reading some new cards you may have heard of – Tarot?"

With this revelation, there followed a deathly silence. I'm sure it was no more than a few seconds but, as there was an obvious tension, it felt like a lifetime. I decided that I might have insulted them somehow. Perhaps it was a matter of their religious beliefs and they were deeply offended? Admittedly, I myself had been wary of the word 'Tarot' initially. There is often a lot of 'bad press' surrounding the idea of Tarot readings, but I have come to know that it is based on a lot of misunderstanding of the true meaning of these cards.

I felt upset as I watched their reactions, and even more so when I saw what I thought to be a tear running down this lovely lady's face. She must have noticed me looking, because they quickly said their goodbyes and went on their way before I had a chance to explain anything further. As they hurried off, I began to feel a deep pain inside and it troubled me. Until that moment, I had been feeling very happy and light.

A few days passed and then one afternoon, while I was watching the shop for Suzie who was on her dinner-break, in walked this lovely couple. As I saw them arrive, I felt a little nervous to be honest and was ready to apologise to them about the cards I had mentioned on our last meeting. But before I could offer any apology or explanation, the wife had already begun to speak.

"Mark," she said gently, "we would really like to speak with you. I've something to tell you;

something we'd both like to share with you. It's about our son." She smiled and yet there was so much sadness in her eyes.

She continued, "Not so long ago, before his sudden passing to the Spirit world, our beautiful son worked on a fish farm in Scotland. He had been there for two years. Each evening at home he would spend time working on something he was very passionate about: the study of ancient Scottish symbolism. He had such love for the ancient mystics that he interpreted and captured some himself through his own personal designs."

She then handed me a silk cloth and within it was a set of seventy-eight Tarot cards which her son had made by hand and painted himself.

I was completely overwhelmed, and felt tears pricking my eyes from the deep emotions I was feeling.

She continued, "After my son's passing, I could never think to throw these cards away and I really wasn't sure what I should do with them....that is, until the other day and the conversation we had then."

She looked at me kindly. "I'm sorry, Mark, for rushing off like that. It's just that we were so overwhelmed when you told us you had started reading Tarot. Somehow I knew our son had guided us to you. These were his passion and I can see you share the same passion; we know he would have wanted you to have them."

It was such an unforgettable moment; I felt completely overcome as we hugged and I gave them a promise that I would cherish their son's cards for the rest of my life.

So often I look closely at these cards. They are truly the most amazing I have ever seen. The detail and artwork deeply reflect how much love and devotion went into them. The result is something utterly priceless.

Today they sit in my psychic studio where they have pride of place, and they always make a special appearance in every workshop I have ever done. To share this most beautiful and amazing story is always such a joy. Even when we move to the Light, Spirit finds a way to get the right outcome.

This story is one which truly touches all who hear it and these beautiful cards will play a big role in my life for ever.

Conclusion

After we leave this world, we continue to be a part of the daily lives of our family and friends. That connection is not lost, even though you may not always feel a presence or think you have ever received a definite 'sign' that they are near. Our loved ones who have passed are always there. How incredible was it that this wonderful Spirit guided his loving mother to gift these amazing cards to someone she knew would truly cherish them? This intervention also presented a powerful message of confirmation that even in Spirit, we still command great power and strength to complete unresolved issues.

"Life can be so very hard when we lose someone
who touches our lives with love, but know this:
they never leave our side.
In this moment of sadness, reconnect to the joy
you shared together, release the fear that you
have become 'separated.'
Begin a spiritual relationship with your loved
ones, moulding two worlds together.
The greatest tribute you can pay them is forever
to shine your light"

Mark Bajerski

Spirit's Messenger

Not so long ago, I was going through a pretty challenging week. I received news that my part in a project – which I'd been looking forward to – had been cancelled, as it had changed direction and my input no longer quite fitted. I was feeling quite sad over the turn of events, and to help shift this mood I headed out for a walk with my dogs to try and clear my mind. Sadly, it didn't seem to be working and I continued to feel very low.

Suddenly, though, everything changed. Out of nowhere, the largest praying mantis I have ever seen appeared. It flew straight at me and landed on my shoulder. Now I'm not sure what you think of such creatures but I nearly jumped out of my skin, terrified that it was going to take a good bite out of me! With my heart thumping, I slowly plucked up a bit of courage and shook my body vigorously to get it off me. With that accomplished, off I ran like the wind!

A bit further on, I had to slow down as I started to laugh uncontrollably over my reaction. It felt like such a release and I thought how funny I must have looked; an apparently grown-up man running crazily away from a 'vicious attack' from a 'deadly' praying mantis. I thought the moment worth sharing and took out my Blackberry, joking about the incident on my Facebook page with friends. I posted a funny update about the 'perils' of living in the mountains of Spain. It was all fun and light-hearted. I love where I live and being part of nature is vital to me; it is where I see and feel so many signs of Spirit, but I did think a praying mantis sitting on my shoulder was taking 'nature' a tad too far! I smiled as I typed up my story, finishing with, *'Spirit, next time you're going to send me a companion, might it please be something a tad less scary looking... a gentle butterfly maybe?'*

The following day, a chat message popped up while I was checking Facebook. A friend of mine had written, "Hey Mark, did you know there is a very spiritual significance to the praying mantis?"

"You're kidding me!" I replied.

"No, not kidding, Mark," my friend replied. "The praying mantis is actually a very ancient sign with a very a spiritual meaning!"

"Wow, please explain!" I answered very excited to learn more.

My friend continued, "The praying mantis symbolises a 'messenger' from Spirit – now, isn't that something?"

I was amazed by this information and quite curious, so I decided to look a bit more into the meaning of the praying mantis. Ancient text tells us that "Mantis" is the Greek word for "prophet" or 'seer,' a being with spiritual or mystical powers. When a praying mantis appears, the 'seer' determines their message. Wow. It suddenly all made sense to me. Immediately a quotation from a friend of mine sprang to mind: 'Often rejection is Spirit's protection.' During those troubled moments on my walk, where I was full of self-doubt and disappointment, Spirit's messenger came and rested on my shoulder. The revelation about the praying mantis helped me overcome my doubts and the message was as clear as day. I could understand that not all projects would be right for me and of course I could *still* share my message. In my heart, my light shines so brightly knowing that this is what I am doing now: sharing that very message with you in this book today.

Conclusion

Imagine this...after months of searching, you finally find your dream home and you do all you can to complete the transaction. All the while, things keep blocking you. No matter how much energy, time and relentless effort you put into it, in the end the deal just falls apart. Naturally, you feel terrible - deeply disappointed. You keep asking the big 'WHY?'

That is, of course, until the day arrives when you find an even better home and suddenly everything just flows into place. Deep inside, you just knew that this was the home you would have: it's not something you can explain - you just knew. Then, you can finally look back and smile. You say, "Hey, I am so glad we didn't get the first home we tried so hard for!"

If you flow in life and trust that everything is as it should be, then - and only then - do you allow Spirit's divine intervention to flow as well.

Remember this the next time you feel like 'fighting' too hard, as perhaps it will be over something or someone that was never meant to be in the first place. Trust - all is as it should be!

"We all share a connection to the universe and Mother Nature.
The gifts and messages provided to us are endless; through nature, we see, we feel and we heal.
Through flowers and trees, the animals and even the smallest creatures with whom we share this earth, Mother Nature provides us with signs and messages about ourselves and the world we live in.
Each moment provides an opportunity for us to learn.
Observe all the 'signs of life'; see what Mother Nature may be telling you"

Mark Bajerski

Buddha Call

One sunny morning I went to the beach with a friend. I needed to spend a little time working with her on my new business cards; the content and colours I would choose etc. I often choose to work by the sea as it is one of the best places where I can still my mind and think clearly. We'll talk about the healing powers of the sea again later on in the book.

On this particular day, things weren't going exactly as I had planned. I was feeling very distracted. Instead of focusing on the sea to gain inspiration, as I usually do, my eyes were being drawn towards the mountains to the left of where I was sitting. Looking up, I was almost blinded by a very sudden bright glare. It was the glorious reflection of the sun as it caught the golden- tip of a 'Stupa', a beautiful Buddhist temple which stood almost at the top of the mountain.

"Wow! Doesn't that steeple look amazing from down here?" I remarked almost dreamily to the lady I was with. I knew of the temple of course, located just a short drive from the mountain pueblo (village) of Benalmadena. I'd not yet been to visit it, though. Now, looking at it, elevated high on the mountain and sparkling in the sunlight, it looked nothing short of majestic.

Over the next fifteen minutes we continued our discussions but I still couldn't summon much enthusiasm to concentrate on thinking about the designs, and I thought it was maybe time to go. That's actually odd for me as I rarely – if ever – lack enthusiasm for any aspect of what I do. Also, the idea that I would feel ready to leave the beach within fifteen minutes of arriving there is unheard of for me. Though she agreed to do so, my friend was more than surprised when I asked if it was okay if we could just call it a day – I didn't feel that I could make any progress by staying there.

As we were walking up from the beach, my eyes continued to be drawn towards the Buddhist temple. I stopped for a moment, taking in all its beauty. It truly was a beautiful sight to behold.

Back in the car, we set off home up the mountain road to my village, Mijas Pueblo. I was chatting away happily with my friend, when she suddenly realised I'd taken a wrong turning.

"Mark, where are we going?' she queried.

"Oh dear," I replied, a bit puzzled myself. Then I remembered I could turn back at the next roundabout so we continued on our drive. Of course, back into our conversation, I forgot to turn back and we continued straight on. My friend soon noticed we were now heading into Benalmadena.

"Mark, you've done it again," she said, laughing. "Oh dear, what's going on with you today!"

By this time, I'd grown a bit cross with myself. *'What is up with you today, Mark?'* I thought to myself.

I really wasn't concentrating at all. Looking ahead, I noticed a familiar sight – the shining gold top of the Buddhist temple again. I couldn't help but smile as I realised that perhaps this was a bit of luck after all. We could turn round by the temple and also have a chance to see it up close.

As we got a bit nearer, we were amazed to find what must have been a hundred or more cars, all heading the same way. A man dressed in Buddhist robes was walking along the roadside and I stopped to find out what was going on.

"Today, my brother, four Buddhist Lamas are here at the temple performing initiations," he replied.

I thought that sounded amazing, but was convinced it must all have finished. "Was it enjoyable?" I asked. He simply smiled – and replied, "Just park on the left. It begins in five minutes."

Just a few minutes later, I found myself walking through a crowd of about two thousand people and straight up to the Lamas, until I was right in front of them. It was so entirely effortless that I knew the Universe had led me there that day, and reserved a place for me in this divine moment to be initiated by four of the wisest living Lamas. To have received this blessing gave me such joy and I recall how my body tingled from the immense happiness I felt – and also from the shock of what had just happened.

The Universe is a truly magical place and one which brings people together in a divine moment in time. This was one of those moments...

Conclusion

I believe Spirit has a plan for each one of us. Spirit will find a way to bring you to the right place for many reasons: an experience, a lesson or a divine encounter. These may be moments filled with great joy or heavy challenges but they all have a purpose which helps us to grow spiritually and eventually, to gain a deeper understanding of how and why we are all here. Learning to trust in the greater plan of Spirit brings about a release and creates a deeper calmness in our lives. Whenever you find yourselves at a crossroads and frozen by the fear of making the 'wrong' decision or choice, let go of that fear and take a leap of faith.

It doesn't matter if you choose left or right – in the end, the light shines brightly both ways and now, this is how I live my daily life. I learned a great lesson from that day: how to trust in the greater plan of the Universe.

"Synchronicity is Spirit's way of giving a helping hand, and leading us to where we need to be.
The most beautiful understanding of this is that not only does Spirit work so lovingly towards helping us achieve enlightenment, Spirit plans these amazing events for us many years before they come to light"

Mark Bajerski

THE WINGS OF SPIRIT

One very hot day, a lovely lady had booked in for a reading with me. As she sat down and drank the chilled, fresh water I left out for her, I smiled and began the reading. Placing her left hand on my table, I placed my hand over hers and went into a deep alpha mode.

(For anyone who may be unsure as to what is meant by 'alpha mode', let me try to explain. 'Alpha mode' is a perfectly peaceful and very safe place to be. It is where you ALLOW yourself to be 'out of' your thinking, to empty your mind and be in a perfect flow with life and all its amazing signs and creativity. You are more 'internally' focused. You might relate it to an experience of daydreaming, when your mind is relaxed and yet you suddenly find great ideas and solutions come through into your conscious state. Indeed 'Alpha mode' is a wonderful place where subtle information comes to us). And so, over the next two minutes, I picked up so much about this lady and was especially tuned into her husband who was in Spirit.

I gently told her that her husband was with us, sending his love and protection. He had a particular

66

message to give to her. I spoke his words to her, saying: "It doesn't matter that you were not on time to
be there." Though this was obviously an extremely
personal message for the lady, I couldn't help but
feel she was expecting to hear something more;
perhaps another message, another confirmation it
really was a message from her husband. I felt that
whatever words followed washed off her like water
off a duck's back. Nothing at all seemed to create a
spark for her, or brought the connection that she
seemed to want so desperately. I could really feel
how hard she was trying and my belief is that her
strained efforts, all the 'trying' to grasp onto something, was actually creating more of a block instead.
When you have lost someone very dear to you, it
takes time to heal and accept.

I continued with her reading and once finished,
I asked her how she was feeling. She answered, saying, "I'd really like to receive some kind of 'sign'
from my husband. I've tried but have not received
any sign since his passing." As she spoke, I could see
that the messages I'd passed on had not really resonated with her. I closed my eyes and quietly asked
for one further sign.

In my studio I have a skylark window, which
I open about to three inches – just enough for a
light breeze to find its way into the room. Within
a few seconds of me closing my eyes, the silence in
the studio was broken by a commotion overhead. I
opened my eyes to a quite unbelievable sight. There
was a fairly plump-looking woodpigeon squeezing
its way through the window. The chances of this
happening, in that very moment I asked for a sign,

were about a million to one! For me, I had no doubt this was Spirit at work: divine intervention.

Once through, our 'visitor' then sat quite deliberately on the metal railings above our heads; it was a strange and beautiful moment and I felt quite overcome. Standing up slowly, I gently took the bird in my hands. I looked into the eyes of the lady and gave her a knowing smile; all the while, the pigeon remained calmly perched on my hand. After what I felt was an appropriate time, I left the room quietly in order to release the pigeon outdoors. My wife Suzie was downstairs and looked up with a surprised expression. 'Don't ask!' I chuckled, with a spring in my step. Suzie never does, bless her. She truly understands how many beautiful things happen in my healing studio. I returned upstairs feeling the joy of what had just happened, and wondering how the woman was dealing with it all. I thought it may have overwhelmed her and I was eager to return and help her if needed. She turned to me as I entered the room and, almost as if nothing at all had just happened, she said to me in quite a pleading tone, "Mark please, just *one* sign from my husband for me?" I was totally taken aback by this reaction, feeling tempted to 'flap' my hands or let out a little 'coooo' Of course I never would - my role is one of understanding and acceptance. When we are ready, we stop thinking in a way of 'what is possible; what isn't possible?' and we simply flow in the moment, accepting all the possibilities happening around us in our divine moment.

On a similar theme, I walked one morning to the village square to meet a gentleman who had an appointment with me for a reading. I remember thinking how 'guru-like' and extremely gentle this man seemed with his long hair, clothed all in white and with a beautiful aura about him – truly angelic. As I shook hands with him I could feel immense love and understanding in his heart.

But despite the sense of peace which surrounded him, this man held a deep sadness, related to his father's lack of understanding and love for him. I had connected to this energy after placing my hand above his and tuning into his life, his feelings and his pain. I gave him several messages which truly resonated with him. After the reading, there was a feeling of much more lightness; a breakthrough from the pain. He gave me a hug and started to leave. Just before he walked out of my door, I heard myself say to him, "You will soon receive a sign from your father." He smiled and thanked me, and despite the pain he had felt previously, his face was now purely a picture of hopefulness.

Within the hour, I received a phone call from this lovely man. He told me that after leaving my healing studio, he had felt quite energised and decided to take a walk round the village. Several thoughts were going through his mind as he recalled the many messages throughout his reading. He had decided to sit outside a quiet café and take a little time to process everything calmly. He wondered about the 'sign' that he was to receive from his father – when and what it might be.

"Mark, right in that very moment, I received my answer," he told me emotionally. "You see, as

I sat there thinking about my father, I was almost thrown off my chair by the most deafening sound – the high-pitched screech of a parrot overhead!"

"I see," I said, not really understanding but happy in the knowledge that it obviously made sense to him.

"Mark," he continued, "my heart was racing. I *know* this was my sign. It was meant for me. One thing I will always remember about my father is his nickname – to his family and friends, he was always known as 'Parrot'. Can you believe it!"

Of course I could and we laughed joyously together. What a beautiful call for me to receive; hearing this lovely man reconnected and so uplifted.

Conclusion

What I have observed over the years is that quite often, in looking too hard for the 'thunderbolt and lightning' signs, we miss the small, subtle signs which are truly meant for us. Those who see their signs are the people willing to remain open and to *believe*.

Faith is something we all hold deep in our consciousness. Clear away the 'noise' and the blocks we create in our everyday life and we then clear the way for our faith to grow and allow the light within us to shine.

You can either believe that the timing of the parrot's screech was pure coincidence or you can trust - as this man did - that he had been led to a café where his father's message was waiting for him.

If we allow ourselves to flow in the moment, Spirit will guide us to where we are meant to be. If we are open to believing that all is as it should be, we will be guided *without thought* to where we need to be.

"We all lose faith sometime or other.
This, too, is part of our journey to
self-discovery.
But the one thing I truly know is that faith
never dies inside your heart and soul.
Re-awaken your flame today and live life as you
were always meant to: in love, in peace and in
balance.
You are amazing!"
Mark Bajerski.

CLIMB YOUR MOUNTAIN

One morning as I was waking up, a vivid picture flashed into my mind. In it, there was a lady dressed in white with long white hair. She was holding her arms open. Her face was kind and she wore a beautiful smile.

"I need your help," I heard her say, although her lips did not move. She spoke directly to my heart and I replied back in the same way, asking, "Tell me, how I can help?"

She smiled and said, "Don't worry, you will soon know what to do and what to say." With that, my eyes opened and I wondered whether I had been dreaming.

As I began to get myself ready for the day, the telephone rang.

A softly spoken lady asked me shakily through her tears, "Hello, is this Mark Bajerski?"

"Yes it is," I replied.

"Um, I'm not exactly sure why I've called," she said. "You see, I've read about you in a magazine and felt I needed to call you." Immediately, I knew that this call was the reason for my dream that morning.

I never push anyone into having a reading or a healing. I believe that choice must come from the person themselves and so I said to this lady, "If it feels right in your heart to come and see me, then my door will always be open to you."

Later that day, a lady with long, dark hair walked into my studio. As she sat down, she wiped her tear-stained eyes and I began to speak to her about her past. Before long, I was tuning into her partner and a lot of information came flowing through. Her partner had been a very warm and kind man when they first met. Sadly, over time, he had slowly turned into a darker side of himself. I was brought more deeply into this man's life and into his energy. As if I had become him, I could see his journey clearly; it had taken him to a dark place where he had started hitting this lady and mentally abusing her.

I was able to share some information which she had not been aware of beforehand. It had been the cause of a great deal of pain for this man: information about his mother who had never shown him any love or attention and of his violent and abusive father, who only had two sides to him - silence or rage. No matter how much this man had tried, his father had never shown any feelings of pride towards his son, right up until he had passed away. This man had desperately wanted a mother and father who loved and supported him, and the fact that they were the complete opposite of that had been a cause of constant struggle and challenge. Unable to let go of the painful relationships he'd had with his parents, and not having sought any way to overcome the pain and anger, he could not face his demons. And because of this, he'd found himself in the same abusive cycle towards his partner as his father had been with him.

As I continued I could see this lady's energy change. It was a moment of divine enlightenment when all the terrible things that had happened to her partner finally made sense. She recognised that she had not been the cause of any of his pain and that he had not really intended to hurt her. Within that moment, she was able to let go of all the questioning and years of guilt.

One hour passed very quickly and the woman who had walked though my door was no longer in front of me. This was a new woman with a renewed inner power and self-confidence. Her light was shining brightly and the final part of my work was about to begin – her healing.

As she lay on my healing bed, I began by clearing the energy of her past, cutting cords and burning all the negative emotions from her mind and stomach. As I did so, she fell into a deep state of peace.

When the healing ended, her eyes opened slowly, full of happiness and a new strength I had not seen there before. I knew my work was done.

"Thank you, Mark," she said. "While I was sleeping I felt a warmth and a trust that I would be okay. I'm now ready to face the world and more so, I *know* what it is I need to do!"

"That's wonderful," I said, feeling much happiness for her. "I wish you well on the next part of your journey."

Some time later, she sent me a message from Italy. She talked about how she had started the climb up her personal mountain and that she was finding happiness inside herself which she hadn't felt since she was a child. Her journey found her meeting some amazing people who treated her with complete respect – something again she had not felt for more than fifteen years. I was truly thankful for the words Spirit had channelled through me; they were able to help this lady begin her personal healing journey.

Conclusion

The timing of this lady coming to my door was, without doubt, Spirit's intervention; a divine, sacred moment where she was able to move forward with trust and belief in her choice of a new start. To explain in words the energy of Spirit's intervention is almost impossible – one must be in the presence of it to truly understand, to truly feel the confirmation that you are seeking. This energy manifests as a higher vibration that you feel deeply within the mind, body and soul and everything comes together, making complete and utter sense. I would like to share one of the most powerful seven words in this world, which I use on a daily basis to help me through the struggles of life. They are: '**No-one has the power over me!**"

An inner strength and bravery to face the challenges which life throws at us exists within each one of us. Spirit recognises your inner pain and gifts you the love and strength to move beyond it – and also the power to reignite your inner flame.

"Trust that your love has more power to change
any situation in and around you.
Today, please allow spirit to help. Stop fighting, let go and believe that in the end, it will all
work out just as it should do.
Trust that you will be smiling; you will be on
top of your mountain looking down and saying,
"YES!"
Love, believe and above all trust that these lessons will make you stronger and happier than
you could ever possibly imagine."

Mark Bajerski

PATHWAY TO FREEDOM

On a rare but welcome rainy day on the Costa, a beautiful lady sat opposite me in my studio.

She looked extremely upset and I felt her pure heart crying out desperately for some help; yearning for a miracle. I looked deeply into her brilliant blue eyes and I could see pure kindness; you could describe her as an 'earth angel,' just as my wife Suzie is to me.

I placed my hand gently over hers and felt so much pain in her heart - perhaps the loss of a loved one? And yet, *No!* I sensed that the man she was so in love with, and for whom she was feeling tremendous pain, had not left this world. It was a bit confusing; as if he were trapped somewhere. With such an unusual and strange feeling about this, I closed my eyes, asking Spirit to show me what I needed to say and do.

I heard myself explain to this lovely lady that the man she loved so much was indeed trapped and lost. He had done something wrong - very wrong in fact, and was suffering greatly for his mistake.

I felt Spirit's smile and words of encouragement started to flow. "Your love is going through a great test of faith. He made a terrible mistake and now knows, deep in his heart, what it is he has done. He is not a bad soul. He knows of love and what is right from wrong. Today you can help him. Today, begin by sending him one spiritual book each week. He will read each book and they will bring him closer to your arms again. Never doubt the power of Spirit and share this message with him in a letter. Soon, a miracle will happen and in time, you will find yourselves together once again."

After the reading and many tears, she bravely shared the story of this man with me.

"Mark, I only met the man you are talking about some months ago. We fell deeply in love and life was beautiful. That was, until the day I found out he'd been arrested. He was taken to prison for being part of a group of men caught trying to bring drugs into the country. He told me that this was the first time he had done anything like this and he has so much regret. He says his life is ruined and there is no point in living. He's probably facing fifteen to twenty-five years in prison."

She paused then for a moment, and sounding a bit brighter, said, "Being honest, somehow your words have truly lifted my heart. I don't know how, but I know and believe you are right. I believe every word you have spoken and today, I will make a promise that each week I *will* send a spiritual book for him to read. I'll also send him a letter to explain everything that was said." It felt so good to hear her sounding uplifted and positive. We hugged and said our goodbyes. Some months went by and then one day, I received an email from this beautiful lady. In it, she told me that she had done exactly what Spirit had asked and sent a book each week. As her love had started to read them, she noticed a truly amazing change in his letters. He had become stronger and a lot more confident that everything would be okay.

"Today is the trial, Mark," her email said. "Please can you pray for him?"

Smiling, I replied saying that if he had indeed read all the books, there would be nothing to worry about but I would send all my love to the judge to ask that he saw the man before him as someone filled with remorse.

Days went by and then I had a surprise visit from this lady. She wanted to come and explain how the day in court had gone. "Mark, as you know, the trial was one where five people were facing fifteen to twenty-five years in prison. I had to come and tell you personally that only four out of the five men were sentenced to prison that day and the fifth – the man I love – was released," she explained through tears of joy and relief. "How can I ever repay you?" she asked with total sincerity, "My partner would very much like to meet you and to thank you personally."

"I did nothing," I replied with a smile on my face. "It was both you and he who made this happen. The lesson he chose to face has been conquered. When you accept in your heart that you have made a mistake and agree never to go down that path again, Spirit sees this and helps by way of showing this energy to the right person. In this case, that person was the judge who could see in your loved one's eyes that he had learned his lesson. That is what set him free."

I did get to meet her love a few weeks later and I can tell you this - the man who stood in front of me was someone who had found his path of enlightenment and could once again breathe air of pure happiness and life.

Conclusion

Even when it seems we have 'lost our way' and could be at our lowest point, if we keep an open heart, Spirit will find a way to bring the tools - or the message - we need into our lives in order to help us back onto our path. How clever was Spirit to bring this lady into this man's life at just the right moment? A lady who would stand by his side and believe in him no matter what, a lady who would carry the message of Spirit from my door and place her trust in that message. That same sense of trust and faith continued on through this man's commitment to reading the spiritual books. He reached a pure, deep, inner understanding about how his life needed to change. I believe this is what enabled him to reach such a different vibration. A pure and higher vibration became this man's new energy; a very positive energy which on the day of the trial, was so profound it was felt by all in the courtroom and, most importantly, by the judge - resulting in this most amazing outcome.

"Who hasn't made mistakes?
Who hasn't wished, at some moment in their
lives, that they could just turn back the clock?
What makes us strong is not the knowing that
every single action we make or do is perfect, it
is realising that we can be wrong and that we
do make mistakes.
When we accept this into our lives, we begin to
see that our journey is not only about the highs,
but also living through and understanding the
lows;
We must learn to accept our actions and open
up to a greater understanding of why we are
here.
Spirit will see this willingness and feel this new
energy inside our hearts;
There is nothing that Spirit cannot do to help
us back along our life's journey, helping us
to recognise and take that next step towards
happiness."

Mark Bajerski

THE GIFT

Just recently, a good friend of mine, Cecilia, surprised with me a very thoughtful gift. It was a bottle
of holy water. I am not religious but I do respect all
faiths and, like all the gifts I receive, I placed this
alongside the healing oils in my studio. Cecilia explained that she just had to get this gift for me. I
smiled as I thanked my dear friend and I didn't question why she felt it 'had' to be holy water; I didn't
give it a second thought really. It touches me when
I'm given a gift and, over the years, I have learned
that Spirit is so very clever in what is brought to my
door.

A number of days later, I received a call from a
beautiful soul who claimed her body was being 'at-
tacked'. I gently asked her not to say another word
– just to come and see me for a healing session. She
was Spanish, and arrived the very next day.

As she lay on the healing bed in my studio, I
placed my hands on her heart and forehead. I knew
instinctively that there was indeed something
causing a great deal of pain within her; I cannot
say what, but it was very real. Moments later, she
began to scream. I don't ever get upset or in anyway

distracted by sudden screams or jerky movements from a person receiving healing – it is not such an unusual occurrence. However, it is not something that everyone will experience. Healing creates a flow and connection of pure energy and each experience is very personal to the individual. My work over the past few years has enabled me simply to flow with the energy in the room and, to date, I have not had a single person who felt in any way 'frightened' by the experience of healing.

As we continued, her entire body was jerking randomly and I noticed her eyelids flicking rapidly. Just then, her eyes opened wide and I felt their intense stare travel deep into my soul. The energy was very forceful. There were roars rising from within her throat, and the jerking became more aggressive as her body was literally being tossed up and down on my healing bed. There was movement inside her throat and spasms throughout her entire body which even a contortionist would find difficult to do. I could feel my hands really burning up and the body of this beautiful soul was dripping wet. I held my smile and kept reassuring her as gently as possible that all was fine. I whispered these comforting words for her to hold onto: "Remember always, the Dark cannot stay where there is Light."

At that moment, I felt myself being gently pushed from behind my back. As I turned, my eyes were drawn directly towards the bottle of holy water Cecilia had given me days before. I found it impossible to focus on anything else. There are many gifts I have been guided to use over the years and suddenly, this connection meant something. I knew then that the holy water had been given - not for me, but in order to help this lady. I would use it to cleanse and clear away this negative energy. Opening the bottle, I poured the water generously over her throat and forehead. Her eyes closed tightly and she screamed loudly *"¡Se Quema!"* (*'It's burning!'*) Despite what you may think, I knew instinctively that her healing was working. Gently, I placed my hands on her heart and forehead and again comforted her by saying "I make this promise to you right now. These hands will not move from your body until you are feeling better."

Although my hands continued to burn, I didn't move them. I focused completely on the light from my hands; this light was burning through the fear and darkness trapped inside her body.

Two hours went by before this lady finally opened her eyes. I could tell immediately that she was 'back'! She looked at me and smiled, like a new person...she looked at peace; she looked very beautiful.

As I arrived home from my studio that evening I felt that familiar warm glow coursing through my body; the knowing that I'd participated in something quite extraordinary and spiritual. With some time to rest, I looked up and gave thanks for the gift of that wonderful day.

Before heading off to bed, I decided to clear my mind of the day's events a bit and to watch a little TV. I sat upright in my chair just as the opening credits of a movie rolled up on the screen *'Warner Bros presents....The Exorcist.'* I smiled knowing 'Spirit' was present and probably winking at me!

Conclusion

Some indeed may view this experience as a kind of 'exorcism'. For me, it was a simple case of cleansing negative energy. What occurred to me most of all about this healing was how it was a gift from a dear friend which played a significant part in the healing of someone who had not yet walked into my life – now that is the power of Spirit and synchronicity at its best!

I am always guided towards which healing oils – and sometimes crystals and other items – with which to work. The 'what' and the 'why' should not play a leading role in our lives; only the knowing that in the end, it is Spirit and light which guide us to a true place of healing. Through letting go of fear, and learning to trust the heart, Spirit and the universe, we invite peace into our lives and receive an awakening to our own divine gifts.

There is nothing that love and light cannot overcome.

"I cannot 'fix' someone; no-one can!
There are many lightworkers who can, however,
show you what you may have forgotten. Once
your amazing flame is burning brightly again,
it's up to you to keep it alight.
No-one can - nor should they - ever live your
life, just as you should not try and live theirs.
Lessons can only be learned by you, and the
feelings you experience make the necessary
changes to bring everything back into its spiritual place."
Mark Bajerski

Accidents Do Happen

On many occasions, I am invited to provide appointments outside my studio. On such a day I was working in a local vitamin shop where I had been asked to come and give some readings.

In the basement of the shop, a lovely table had been set out for me, dressed very nicely with candles. Before long, my first client of the day came down the stairs. He was quite a tall man who wore a broad smile on his face but I sensed that this smile was somewhat forced.

Naturally, I smiled back to welcome him and shook his hand. I began the reading, speaking about his personality, his work and what the future would hold. The further we got into his reading, I began to feel quite a deep pain in my body. I looked into this man's eyes and stopped the reading abruptly. I asked him directly, "All of this, all my words, they don't mean a single thing to you, do they?"

He looked at me and said, "Mark, I'm sorry but, yes, that's true." I never force my work on anyone but I really didn't want to give up. I needed to get to the cause of this deep pain I was sensing. Closing my eyes I remained quiet and just asked for help.

'*Please*,' I thought, '*can anyone help me? Please help me find the way to heal the pain inside this kind man's heart.*'

Within seconds, I had a vision. A picture came forth of a young man; he had been involved in a high-speed crash which had immediately taken him into the spirit world. "Dear sir," I said gently and with much care, "I see an accident; a young man involved in a crash and this person has been taken to Spirit."

I opened my eyes and felt my tears coming as the man replied with such emotion, "That was my son. At the age of twenty-one he was taken from me. I just want to understand *WHY*? Why did he travel so fast on a motorbike? Why did he crash? I need to understand WHY?"

Closing my eyes again, I simply asked. What followed is truly divine and left me with a renewed belief in the 'why and how' we can leave this world. This had indeed been an 'accident' and the message from his son was very clear.

"This accident was my fault. I was travelling far too fast. I made a fatal mistake and I carry that burden with me each day. Father, every day I see your pain, my sister's pain and that of all my friends. I WAS NOT MEANT TO LEAVE THIS WORLD. It was not 'divine timing'- it was a mistake; *MY MISTAKE*. Father, please forgive me and tell everyone how much I love and miss them with all my heart. The day *you* find happiness will be the day I find *my* happiness. I love you and will always be with you."

It had been a highly emotional reading for both of us, after which we hugged quietly and said our goodbyes.

A few weeks on, I received a phone call from a lady who was selling her home and wanted a house cleansing. I agreed, asking her not to give any details about the house or any issues attached to it.

On the day I arrived at the house, I found myself in her living room and my eyes were drawn quite suddenly to the photo of a young man. I received a message and immediately knew this young man had passed to the Spirit world. For whatever reason, he wasn't happy with this photo being kept on the mantelpiece. He didn't seem to want it to be there.

I moved on with the cleansing to see what further pieces to the puzzle I could find. As soon as I got to one of the bedrooms there was an immediate feeling of sadness and the vibration in the room was also very low. I knew that of all the rooms in the house, (and there were many!) this was the room of the young man in the photo. Now, I began to put more of the pieces together.

Sitting on the bed, I closed my eyes. The lady who owned the house had needed to go out but told me that her husband would return home shortly. Quite honestly, I was glad to have this time alone. With no distractions, it would be easier for me to find out what I needed to know. I hoped the young man in the photo would speak through me and bring answers to those who most needed to heal.

It wasn't long before I could feel his thoughts coming through and tears began to stream down my face. I was given the message that it was time to clear out his room and would his father please give all his collectables to his best friends; he really wanted this to happen. I turned and looked out of the window. I must have stood there for what seemed like ten minutes, crying at the beautiful view of the mountain. This young man really missed this view and the ability to look up at his mountain as he so often did, thinking about what he wanted to do when he got older. I got the sense then that his death had been very sudden.

Leaving the room, I went downstairs again and into the kitchen. In this room, I felt drawn to a corner just under the stairs. I couldn't explain why, but I immediately felt at peace in that corner and decided to sit there for a while. As I did so, a deep feeling of peace washed over my body - so much so, that I could feel my eyes becoming heavy and beginning to close. I was feeling utterly relaxed when suddenly, the kitchen door opened and in walked a tall man I assumed to be the owner's husband. I realised then that he was someone I already knew: he was the gentleman who had received the reading at the vitamin shop a few weeks earlier. Although he expected me to be at his home that day, it occurred to me how bizarre I probably looked, sitting alone under the stairs. What on earth was this man going to think of me? With a bemused look on his face, he asked, "Mark why are you sitting down there??"

Looking up, I told him truthfully, "Actually, I have no idea why, but I just feel quite happy here."

He raised his head and just said, "Oh, well, that's very strange."

I got up quickly, asking if I could explain to him what I had learned from the cleansing and what could be done to help the energy in the home. We began back in the living room and I explained, as kindly as I could, that the photo on the mantelpiece should be moved. Again, I heard this man repeat the same words, "Oh, very strange."

We then headed upstairs to the bedroom. Entering the room, I again felt such sadness and explained this feeling. "The energy in this room is very sad and very low. I was given a message that all these collectables are to be given to your late son's best friends."

It was the third message and the third time this man's wistful reply was simply, "Oh, very strange."

Looking out of the window then, I finished by saying, "Your son used to spend a lot of time looking out of this window, wondering and dreaming about what his life would be like." With that, we left the room quietly and went back downstairs. Back in the living room, he sat down and proceeded to tell me everything.

"Mark, the other week a lady arrived here looking to buy this house. As soon as she entered the living room, she explained to us that she is a medium and that this picture doesn't want to be there!" he said, pointing to the picture of his son. "The very same picture you've advised us to move."

He continued, "The items in my son's room; I had already made plans to give them to all his friends but just couldn't find the right time. I suppose now must be the right time, then?" I could really feel the emotional pull this was causing him

DIARY OF AN ACCIDENTAL PSYCHIC

- between such sadness and finally finding a way to let go.

"And the kitchen?" he said with a sad smile, "that very place where you sat at the bottom of the stairs? As a young boy, that was the *only* place my son spent his time playing in this house. He could always be found there. He'd say it was the one place in this house where he always felt most happy."

Conclusion

Whatever we go through in our lives, and however we might feel about going through the experience of this life here on earth, we should always remember that we are the lucky ones! We are so blessed to live an earthly life; grasp this experience with both hands for the time we have here is just a moment. Embracing life and living it to the full with an open, kind and forgiving heart, we can come to understand the purpose of our lives. Yes, we are blessed; yes, we are protected.... but we must never forget the 'golden rule' and that is: we are all given choices in our lives. Just as we have the choice to live a peaceful life, we also have a choice to do incredible harm to others. We have the choice to get into a vehicle and travel at a safe speed. If we live dangerously, however, and go beyond normal safety levels, we put our own lives and the lives of others in danger. This is when accidents may occur. As the above story confirms, not everyone's moment of moving to the light is down to 'divine timing' – quite simply, my belief is that accidents do happen. It is vital that each one of us truly values the gift of life and that we take responsibility for our actions; understanding that there will always be consequences which we have to live with, and that those consequences may well bring a great deal of pain into someone else's life as well.

We know we are protected by Spirit, but this does not mean we don't need to look left and right when crossing the road! I can tell you of my own recent story where by not living in the moment, I had to bear some painful consequences. Too preoccupied by where I needed to be and at what time I needed to be there, I rode my motorbike at a nifty 50mph down a dangerously wet road. Not surprisingly, I found myself flying through the air. I cracked a few bones in my shoulder, and ended up taking a journey to the hospital which put an end to any of those plans I had been fretting about! Even in the spirit world, we can see our mistakes and we can truly understand why accidents can and do happen.

"My heart has always been filled with love,
It is what I have been through that makes me
feel the way I do today.
I am still the same as I was before, only now I
have seen so much and felt so much.
In the end, I have always been - and always
will be - the same heart. That can never change;
deep inside my heart is love..."
Mark Bajerski

Pushy Spirit

One year, my wonderful mother-in-law flew from Huddersfield to Malaga with a friend for a holiday. I picked them up from the airport and took them to their hotel nearby. Later on that evening, I began to feel a bit 'strange.' I mentioned to Suzie that something felt a little wrong with me, but I honestly couldn't explain what that was.

By nightfall, I felt very agitated - almost angry. As time passed, this feeling of anger was getting gradually worse. The most disturbing part was that I felt unable to control it; it was as though something was taking over my thoughts. I don't mind admitting that it really began to scare me. I didn't know what I should do. I considered calling the doctor and then decided he would probably just laugh and prescribe me a couple of Valium!

As I struggled to understand what was happening, I felt a severe pain to the side of my stomach. It remained quite fierce for some time. At the same time, I started to feel that perhaps someone was trying desperately to communicate with me through the pain and anger in my own body. I'm sure this all sounds pretty crazy and, trust me, it was a real battle for me to remain calm; so many frightening possibilities were going through my mind. I just could not understand what was happening to me or why.

Determined to not frighten Suzie with all of this, I went quietly upstairs. I thought to sit for a while in the stillness of a dark room and try to 'listen' to what was going on inside me, hoping I might get some answers. Sure enough, as I did this, the presence of a young man came through. It felt certain he was very angry about his life, over all the 'bad luck' he'd suffered and wrong choices he had made. It was as though he had left our world by his own actions. Whatever the remaining issues, I felt this man's deep anger and knew he was not in a peaceful place. I knew all this was true because internally, I was taking quite a beating myself; the pain in my own body had intensified and I was feeling much worse than before.

As the pain deepened, more information came through to me. I learned much of what I needed to know – apart from WHO he needed to talk to and WHY. A sudden flash of Suzie's mother came into my mind, together with a recollection of a story Suzie had told me of her mum's friend who had lost her son. I couldn't help but wonder if this was the same lady who had arrived that day to Spain with my mother-in-law? Running downstairs, I asked Suzie directly. Looking at me with much concern she replied, "Yes it is. But why do you ask, Mark?"

"I'm not a hundred per cent sure, Suzie." She could tell that, too, from my expression but I continued, "I really don't feel very good, quite honestly, and I think that someone is trying to connect with me from the Spirit world. My feeling is that it's not a good message. Is it okay for you to tell me what you know about this lady's son?"

Suzie told me all she knew. It seemed this man had been unlucky in life and, many times, had found himself falling into trouble. At some point when he was about forty years old, alcohol finally took him to the other side.

What Suzie told me made perfect sense and I was certain that this was the Spirit of the lady's son. More importantly and, with much relief, I understood it was *his* anger manifesting itself through me. The pain I was experiencing in my side was, in fact, his liver damage!

I battled with this man's Spirit for the rest of the night; it was one of the worst nights of my life. I can stand a lot of pain, having suffered from irritable bowel syndrome for thirty-eight years, but I was in a very poor state by morning. Though it was painful, I knew I had to hold myself together and not allow this spirit to take me over. If I had allowed this to happen, *I* would have become angry and aggressive too. I would have rushed off to find his mother and tell her everything – but, despite the pain, I understood this was not the right thing to do. This was *my* fight and I would not allow him to bully me as had been his way in his life here. The message he wanted me to pass on to his mother was very forceful: in effect, he wanted me to take his anger to her.

Possibly if I'd told his mother everything it might have made things a bit clearer for her, but I was listening to my heart on this and I knew that it was not what it wanted me to do. Instead, I started by ordering this energy to leave my body; telling it that forcing itself on someone was very wrong – this was not the way or the time. Try as I might, however, I finally had to accept I was way out of my depth. I was deeply enmeshed in something I didn't fully understand and which, quite frankly, was scaring me to death.

I rang a friend of mine who I felt could help. As I began to explain what was happening, she told me to come round to her home immediately. I didn't need to be told twice! On my arrival, she told me to sit in a chair she had prepared for me. There were two other ladies in the room with her and the room had been prepared by burning sage; a wonderful herb with healing properties and which has an amazing, calming effect on negative energy. My friend took control of things and began to address the Spirit of this man directly herself.

I felt my entire being was taken over. This Spirit knew it was the final round now and an anger rose inside me that I have never before experienced in my life (and never wish to experience again!). I literally wanted to throw punches at everyone in the room – it felt insane. Three loving ladies were working to banish this pushy spirit from my body and I was struggling fiercely just to stop myself from swearing at them like a crazy man. I could hear my friend's voice speaking to me and I answering back, but they were not my words – rather the words of the young man. Simply put, I was present in the room but I was definitely taking a back seat. Answers were coming out of my mouth that just weren't my words.

This frightening ordeal continued for about thirty minutes. Finally, I'm so grateful to say that whatever my friend and the other ladies had done, had worked. Slowly, the pain went and I felt a familiar calmness return. As I recovered, they suggested I leave the room, to go outside the house and rest a while there. Shortly afterwards, my friend followed me out. "Are you okay?' she asked in a concerned voice.

"No!" I replied, a bit shortly. "Can you please explain what on earth that was all about?"

She sat down beside me and began to explain as gently and as best she could. "Mark, in our particular field of work, we become magnets to any Spirit. It's actually quite an important lesson to learn who we allow 'in' and how close we want them to come." After what I'd just been through, I didn't much like what I was hearing; it really scared me.

I heard myself saying, "Look, I didn't *want* or *ask* for any of this to happen to me! I just want *out!*" My friend didn't argue. Instead she pointed out to me that whatever way I would decide to take this experience, it had happened in order to serve as a *LESSON* for me. In order to understand more about those who move to the Spirit world, I needed to go through this or another similar experience. It was the only way I could learn how to control these occurrences in both myself and in others. It had been meant to happen.

Though still quite shaken from the experience, I sat there for a while until I could see how her words made good sense. The more I relaxed, the more I felt myself accepting the lesson.

I turned a corner that night. Looking back, I am grateful for this important lesson – one which helps me to share many spiritual experiences with people in my work today.

Conclusion

Whatever path in life we are on – whether a doctor, lawyer, parent, artist – we will always face challenges and fears about our choices.

"Am I good enough? Can I see this challenge through? Is this really for me?" Facing a particular challenge is often Spirit's way to help us overcome our fears and in doing so, allows us to understand and embrace all aspects of our vocation. These 'successes' lead us to a stronger and higher level of understanding about our life and 'the journey'. We learn from our experiences and, in turn, we can share those learned lessons in order to help others along their chosen paths too.

Whatever our path, we should never force our gifts onto anyone – *including* anyone in Spirit, just as those in Spirit should not force any of their unresolved issues onto us. If this Spirit had come to me with love, respect and understanding, then without any doubt in my heart, I would have done everything in my power to have given the messages needed to his beautiful mother and help resolve the situation.

However, where intense anger and rage exists, being 'bullied' is not something we should ever have to accept. Mutual respect between all on earth and in Spirit is so important to our development on our spiritual path.

"Even in my darkest moments I have learned many great lessons.

I am thankful for every single one of those lessons, for I have become a more understanding and loving man.

Every one of those dark moments has made me who I am today.

The real secret of why we are here is to be open and always know that our most painful paths can be the greatest goals for our higher understanding and allow us to reach a new, higher vibration.

Remember my dear friends; we see the light best when in darkness."

Mark Bajerski

HEAL ONE, HEAL MANY

One beautiful, sunny day I was enjoying my morning coffee at the Danish centre in the village where I live. A lady sitting behind me asked suddenly, "Excuse me, but are you Mark Bajerski?"

"Yes," I said to her and turned to see a lady with long, dark hair and a grin that seemed to say, '*I know something you don't know!*'

"May I sit with you for a moment?" she asked.

"Umm, well yes," I said, feeling increasingly curious.

"My name is Becky," she said as she sat at my table. "You don't know me, but you know my husband, Adam. You gave him healing a few months ago."

"Oh yes," I replied. "I remember Adam, how is he?"

"Great!" she replied, but her next statement really surprised me. "Actually, the healing you did on him even managed to heal our dog!"

"Your *dog*?" I replied, feeling pretty confused. After all I'm a psychic and as far as I know, not Dr Doolittle!

Becky went on to explain exactly how life had changed after I gave Adam pure energy healing.

"One evening we were all at home together – Adam and I with our two children Emma and William, and Toby, our cocker spaniel," she said. "We watched TV for a while and I put the kids to bed; all completely normal. Once the kids were settled in their beds, I went back downstairs and noticed something very odd. The TV had been switched off and Adam was sitting at the table looking straight at me. I felt a bit nervous as I asked him what was going on. He explained that he'd been to see a psychic three weeks before that night and had received a healing to deal with the way he'd been feeling." She explained that they had then spent five hours talking about Adam's past and that for the first time in twelve years, she could make sense of all the sadness her husband had been carrying.

"The following day I kept thinking about what he'd said and a pure and deep love I have for Adam returned – a love that had sadly slipped away a bit over the years. I remember smiling to myself all the while I washed up that day. Even when Emma collided with my leg I automatically turned and asked if she was OK, and gave her a kiss; normally, I would have shouted at her but on this day I didn't, and it suddenly hit home that I felt HAPPY! I sat with Emma for an hour helping her with a school painting project. As I cooked dinner later I noticed something else different about the family. Emma and William usually either fight or ignore one another completely, but on that day, they sat together and Emma HELPED William draw a picture, encouraging him all the way! When they'd finished painting I paid close attention to their masterpieces and they left the living room feeling really proud." Her eyes were tearing up joyfully as she continued. "When dinner was ready, I decided not to shout for them to come downstairs and instead I went up to their rooms. Emma sang happily when I told her dinner was on the table and, as I walked into William's room, to my utter amazement, I saw he was reading a book to Toby, our dog! There wasn't a single sign of him tugging or pulling at Toby's tail like he usually did – they were two best buddies together. While we ate dinner, Toby rolled over and fell into a deep sleep." It was such a cheerful story that I have to admit, I felt quite overwhelmed. Then Becky let out a beautiful laugh, saying, "So, you see, Mark, your healing didn't just help Adam find the strength to open up his heart to me, the healing also helped ME rekindle my love, understanding and patience towards my husband and children. In turn my children have healed THEIR differences with each other, and last but not least TOBY has found a new best friend in William. We honestly couldn't be happier!"

Conclusion

I constantly see how energy healing is, without question, a life-changing experience. Not only does it benefit the person receiving the healing, but also everyone in that person's life. Those benefits can, quite literally, stretch out for miles. A true healer knows you already have all that you need in order to shine; it is all within you. At times, the stresses of life can dim our inner flame. Once that flame is re-lit, however, you regain a tremendous energy which can be felt further than you could ever imagine and that's when magic happens. An example could be a new job offer which you always wanted, or the love you thought you'd never find walks into your life. The stronger you are within, the more people are drawn to your amazing energy, *wanting* to be around that energy. They will and *DO* feel better. Who wouldn't want to share in that?

"True healers flow naturally onto your path
when they're needed the most,
They shine their beautiful light into your hearts
to re-ignite your beautiful flame.
True healers show you your true inner self, your
true colours and all your gifts, so that you can
continue to follow your dreams,
True healers gently still your mind and
strengthen your heart.
They help you see what exists deep within you
and show you how to allow your self-realisation
to flow.
True healers help you connect with your old,
spiritual wisdom and trust again that you ARE
going the right way; whichever path you walk
will be perfect.
True healers will always help YOU to become
the power over your paths and YOUR choices"
Mark Bajerski

THE WAY HOME

One hot summer's night, I was out walking my two dogs when I decided to take a new walking trail. It was no more than a dirt track and I started to wonder what had possessed me to take this dark, dirty and pretty spooky path, yet all the same, I found myself heading further uphill.

Large trees surrounded us and the moonlight cast curious shadows across the bushes and large rocks that were dotted about us. An eerie silence filled the thick, night air. The track became steeper with both sides of the road flanked by the surrounding mountains.

I had an uneasy feeling that someone was watching me and a chill ran down my body. Within seconds, my ears 'popped,' followed by a whistle in my right ear. Daisy and Denis, my two loyal dogs, were taking quick, short breaths - much as they do when they sense another dog or a cat. They were staring up at the steep mountain on my left which was heavy with trees and darkness. It was almost as though they sensed someone or something was up there. I couldn't let them go because I was afraid they would run off, so I made them sit and I stilled my mind and closed my eyes.

As I tuned into the darkness, I had an over-whelming feeling that someone was crying out for help. I shouted out, "*Is anyone there?*"

Though the feeling of some kind of 'presence' became stronger, there was no reply to my cries. After a short time had passed, I decided to call it a night and go home with the dogs. I could return again on my own.

The very next evening I decided to go back. For some reason, I knew I had to, and see what I could pick up; maybe it was something spiritual. I had been taken there to begin with and it made sense to see it through. With the sensations I'd felt through my body and the whistling in my ears, I had a pretty good indication that Spirit had been near and I needed to be sure.

As I headed back up the mountain track it wasn't long before I found myself at the very same spot and within just a few moments, my ears popped once again. As it had done the night before, a cold feeling washed over my body and with this new energy, I decided to walk off the track to just sit still and 'listen.'

Feelings of a 'Spirit' energy coursed through my body and I decided I should continue upwards into the thick of the mountain trees. As I went higher, the energy became stronger and stronger and although my senses felt a little out of synch, it was not long before things started to come to-gether. Within the stillness and to the left of where I was standing, I tuned into a female spirit. The connection of energy became very strong and I felt her pain; it was as though she had remained trapped in this very spot for what seemed like forever. Details of what had happened to her began to flow through. She had not had an easy death; it was fast and most unexpected. She revealed to me what she looked like and her clothes were from the period of the Moors and Christians, the *Reconquista*.

I sensed a second energy: that of a male in his late twenties. He also appeared to be trapped on this mountain. Then a third energy was felt - another male, older this time, perhaps in his forties. I sat in the darkness with not one, but *three* Spirits trapped between two worlds. At that time, I had no real experience of what I should do. Instead I just asked all three what they wanted. Their responses were not very helpful as they all agreed that they themselves really had no idea - because they had become somehow 'trapped', they had no idea or sense of time, who they were or where they had been before. It was I who appeared to have the information they needed; it was just a matter of putting it all together.

I spoke with each Spirit in turn to explain the '*where*' and the '*why*' and, most importantly, '*how*' they could move forward to 'the Light'. With each story explained, each Spirit was in acceptance about moving forward.

On what became another remarkable night in my life, I remained there with them for a good many hours until all three Spirits had moved into the light. This beautiful experience gave me a stronger understanding about the Spirit world and my connection to it. Ever since then, I happily answer requests from those seeking my skills in working with Spirits.

Conclusion

A Spirit can become trapped in a place of doubt or confusion and leave this world without an intention to move into the light. We have heard of this phenomenon happening in many places: homes where lights turn themselves on and off, a water tap starts running by itself, footsteps are heard around the house or sounds and voices come from a certain – empty – room. Moving between two worlds, these Spirits may at times still feel 'alive' and very attached to the earthly world. This may appear a bit unnerving and somewhat 'spooky,' but if you do happen upon such an experience, don't be over alarmed. What I call this phenomenon is a 'Spirit in Denial'. Working in a loving way, I see and feel how important it is to flow with love and understanding. These beautiful souls are just like you and me. They are caught between our earthly world and the spirit world. Deep inside their souls, what they truly need is to find their way 'home.'

"No matter where we are in the realms of the universe,
WE ARE ALL ONE.
We should always look for ways to help each other"
Mark Bajerski

ACCIDENTAL PSYCHIC – TAKE TWO!

Six years ago, had anyone said to me, "Mark, I'm going to pack you up and settle you down in the Spanish Andalucian hills, in a little shop high upon a mountain, in a tiny room at the top of some winding stairs and we will see who Spirit brings to you!" I would have said, "Ha! You've got to be joking, right?" I know it sounds like a scene from the movie 'Field of Dreams', but this is exactly how my life proceeded to flow – at amazing speed and with many miracles happening on a daily basis.

When you find your true purpose, the vibration and energy you emit are infinite. They have their purpose too and the universe has a magical way of drawing those people into your life who have a need to connect with that vibration.

A perfect example of this was one evening when I received a Skype message from someone in the USA asking for friendship and a reading. Although it was late in the evening, I had finished two full energy-healing sessions and was feeling very uplifted. Happy to accommodate, I decided to do the reading there and then.

What a surprise it was when I learned the caller was in fact a film director based in Hollywood and he was asking me questions such as, *"What do you think of Jude Law in my next blockbuster movie, Mark? How about Christian Bale? OK, and what about Cate Blanchett?"*

There was a time indeed when making such a connection would have blown me away. To think that here I was in my little studio in the village of Mijas, sharing messages from Spirit with a top film director in Hollywood! Nowadays, I'm happily accustomed to receiving calls and messages from people all over the world and from all walks of life. Such is the desire of Spirit.

Once all the answers were given to this director, I ended the reading and off I went home. My wife Suzie, knowing it had been a long one, asked me how my day had gone. I turned to her, smiled and said, "Suzie, you wouldn't believe me if I told you!" ...all the while thinking to myself "If only *Jude Law* knew what I had seen..."

Conclusion

The universe is truly amazing; it holds no barriers, distance or time. We all have gifts and talents which have a purpose in helping others. You could be living in the foothills of Scotland, the outback of Australia or even the mountains of India. Spirit always finds a way - no matter where we are - of bringing the right people together: the pupil and the teacher, the giver and the recipient, the question and the answer.

Many of us are working for the higher good of mankind. Even in the darkest places of the world, if we hold a divine message that will help others gain or reawaken their faith, Spirit will ensure that message will be heard. Synchronicity has a beautiful way of bringing us all together.

"Magic happens every day!
Today, open your heart and mind and allow
Spirit to work her magic."

Mark Bajerski

Angels Come When Needed The Most

One evening, I answered the phone to a very distressed lady. "Is that Mark Bajerski?' she asked anxiously.

"Yes it is," I replied quickly.

"Mark, I really need your help; my daughter is suffering so very much. We have tried everything and she continues to get worse. I am very worried what might happen if she cannot find some kind of peace."

I stopped the caller at this point, explaining that it is better if I don't know any further details. It is how I work and this method ensures that the truth and light come through; I do not bring any confusion into a reading or healing from prior knowledge in my mind.

The following day, mother and daughter arrived at my studio. The moment I greeted them I knew I had to speak to the daughter on her own. I could also tell instantly that she was an 'old soul'. I identify an 'old soul' as a person who has been to this world many, many times. Characteristically, they are calm, sensitive, loving, caring, passionate, creative people and they have a deep sense of always wanting to help. This was confirmed by the amazing energy which flooded the room as we entered my studio. Looking deep into her eyes, I saw a very special girl: one who needed a little love and understanding to help with issues that had taken their toll on this beautiful, young girl. She needed a reminder of who she was, for it was clear that she had forgotten. I explained in loving words that sometimes, being a sensitive and empathic person can make it difficult to understand the actions of others and her journey is one of much greater importance.

I explained to her that she is an 'earth angel' – someone who shines a light for others to see – and what that means in terms of her path. I helped her to see that the challenging time she was dealing with was indeed a hard test but, as she had very special qualities, it was a time she would be able to handle and all would be well. All the while, this girl was nodding her head in agreement. As an old soul, she had always understood, but she just needed the confirmation. Tears were flowing from her eyes – you could feel tremendous healing taking place. She could feel the energy of Spirit in the room and she knew she was in safe hands. I had seen what was going on in her life at that very moment and she believed me when I told her that everything would be fine. She smiled and I knew the words had touched her heart. I asked if I could call her mother in to join us; she smiled again and agreed. As her mother sat down, it was such a relief for her to see that a huge weight and pressure had been lifted from her child.

It was then time to begin the pure energy healing for her daughter. As she lay on my healing bed, I placed my healing oil on her forehead. Within seconds there was a dramatic change of vibration in the room. It was so intense – as if the room were on fire. At this point there was no doubt in my mind – Spirit was in the room and about to come close.

I was seated at the top of her head, her body stretched out in front of me. From there, I could check her chakras and the energy flowing down to the tips of her toes. I felt and saw something then that I had never felt before in all my years as a healer.

At the foot of the bed, hovering over the feet of this beautiful girl, were three dazzling-white orbs of light. I was completely mesmerised and uplifted. I felt total peace, joy and a pure emptiness; the feeling of everything being exactly as it was meant to be – complete perfection. I had never experienced that feeling before and it is something I now work towards achieving every day.

I turned round to see how her mother was reacting to the orbs. I was again amazed by what I saw. Her head was bowed down against her chest with her eyes closed, but her left hand was raised above her head and her finger was pointing directly at the orbs! I was totally awestruck and almost tempted to wake the mother up to confirm that I wasn't going crazy. It struck me, however, that her outstretched arm was confirmation enough that what was happening in this divine moment was very real. It also seemed it was meant for my eyes only. Had Spirit intended it, then she, too, would see - if not, then so be it.

About an hour had passed and the healing session ended with the orbs slowly disappearing. I asked the young girl to open her eyes slowly and sit up. Her mother was crying gently as she asked what had happened. She said that she had felt herself fall asleep but also that her arm was being lifted - though she couldn't raise her head.

I smiled and said, "Don't question this. Look up and say 'thank you', for we have had some beautiful help today."

It was then time for the mother to have healing. Very calmly, her daughter sat down in my comfy chair, got out a book and started writing in it as if nothing had happened. The healing for her mother was quite intense because of what her daughter had been going through. When the healing had ended, we hugged and I turned to her daughter. My eyes were drawn to the book she was writing in. To my surprise, I realised she had not been writing, but sketching an image. For the third time since this girl arrived, the powerful presence of Spirit was once again confirmed. Her sketches were of beautiful angels.

I asked the girl, "Where do you copy these pictures from?"

She replied, "From nowhere- they just come into my mind."

As it is always with synchronicity, the helping hand of Spirit, I know this wonderful girl is here to raise the vibration of angels and the light in this world. I felt incredibly blessed and humbled that Spirit had appeared so vividly to me on that day with her; a divine moment which is imprinted on my soul. It has completely changed my life. It was a turning point and since then, I have never questioned or doubted the power and miracles of Spirit.

Conclusion

There will always be times in our lives when we need a helping hand; none of us is an exception to seeking this universal love.

Do not be fooled by the term 'emptiness'. When we 'empty' our minds, we clear away our fears, doubts and worries and in that divine moment we can connect to the 'one-ness', allowing the power of Spirit to flow through us.

We are all equal and we all deserve Spirit's helping hand. You are no different to the lady I write about and if you truly sit and think for a moment, you may have a flashback to a divine moment when Spirit touched your soul. If not today, then perhaps tomorrow this reminder will come. For me, this divine moment not only healed any doubt that I really am working with Spirit but it confirmed to the three of us, through our own personal experience on that day, that Spirit truly exists. Faith is a personal relationship. Spirit comes to you – not to the masses or the media. Faith is your spiritual path; one of your greatest lessons throughout all experiences in this world. From birth to death, did we hold onto our faith? Did we continue to believe? We are always being given signs and sparks of divine moments to help us hold onto our faith.

Our own faith is the only thing that remains pure in this world; it remains pure in our souls.

"Watching over us are many beautiful Spirits, helping us as far as our path allows. Ultimately, we each have our own divine path of learning - it is the reason why we are here. Spirit knows how much they can help without interference in our challenges.
Often, as we go through many challenges, Spirit gently guides us to the right place where we find beautiful souls who have experienced the same or similar challenges or who may be a channel for Spirit at the very moment when they are needed."
Mark Bajerski

THE HEALER AND THE TREE

Some years ago, as Spirit began to pull me gently onto this path as a healer and spiritual messenger, I found myself out walking my dogs along a certain road leading out of our village. On this route is a magnificent olive tree. I'm sure it must be a couple of hundred years old and the sight of it truly captivated me. In spite of it not being in the most beautiful place – it is smack in the middle of a pavement – its magnitude and magnificence are nonetheless incredibly striking. It amazed me that someone had the sense to not cut it down but instead, to build the pathway around it.

What was quite extraordinary is that the hairs on the back of my neck and head literally stood up on end every time I passed by this tree. The first time I experienced this curious reaction, I looked upwards, expecting to see electrical pylons overhead. Surprisingly, there was not one cable in sight. Why and how this could be happening really puzzled me; it was as if the energy was coming from the tree itself. One day, I decided to sit down on the large roots at the bottom. Instantly, I felt a beautiful warmth wash over my body. It took me a little by surprise but was so relaxing that I closed my eyes and sat there for quite a time. In no time at all, this became a daily ritual for me.

My life was becoming much busier with many people coming to see me from all over the world, and I was providing many more healing sessions. After each busy day was done, I would pay a visit to 'my tree' and just sit and relax in its energy for a bit. I found these daily visits had started to reawaken my deeper love for – and connection with – Mother Nature.

As this bond grew, I felt drawn to place the palms of my hands upon the tree – the energy felt incredible and I recognised the sensation immediately as that of healing. Admittedly, I felt a bit odd standing there with my hands holding onto a tree – I worried that in our little Spanish village, I might compromise my position and reputation as a 'normal' family man and that I'd be labelled a 'hippy/ flower power' or 'tree hugger!' In those early days, that kind of reaction bothered me. I'd try to look less conspicuous; make it seem as though I was waiting for someone or trying to balance myself as I tied my shoelaces. All that changed, though, when one particular day, a small, elderly Spanish lady passed by as I had my hands placed on the tree. I had no time to react and it was a wonderful surprise when she smiled widely and said, *"Mucho energia!"* (*'A lot of energy!'*) I was gobsmacked as I giggled "Si, mucho!" back to her. Ever since then, I never worried about laying my hands on that tree ... and more magic was yet to come!

One evening, just as I went to sit at the tree, I took a call from a friend of mine. I began telling her how I was feeling quite run down after a number of weeks filled with healing sessions.

"Mark, my dear, you need to find yourself a tree," she said.

"A *TREE*?" I replied with much surprise and curiosity.

"Yes, Mark, a tree! Many Shamans believe that as they become more enlightened, they are led to a tree with which they form a spiritual bond - an agreement with one another. The Shaman agrees to take all the negative energy from anyone who is led to his or her door and in turn, the tree agrees to take all that negative energy away from the Shaman; it is a very beautiful ritual."

"*Wow!*" I said in total dismay, "you're probably not going to believe me but *I HAVE MY TREE*! In fact, I'm sitting at *MY TREE* right now!"

In that moment, everything made sense to me and I understood why I had felt drawn to this wonderful tree and created such a loving bond.

Conclusion

Rediscovering 'ME' through nature has not only touched my heart deeply, it has also enabled me to bring more balance into my life. That balance means I wake up without fear or worry and I simply let go of the *'what ifs?'* which so often consume our minds. And so, my wonderful friends, the only possible conclusion is to present you with a gift. As I share my secrets with you in order to receive pure healing from Mother Nature, you will start to bring more peace and balance into your daily lives: find *YOUR* tree and therefore find *YOUR* balance.

Mark Bajerski

"We are all living energy; we are all part of Nature; we are all connected to our Mother Earth.
Awakening to this connection is part of our
destiny.
Once we realise there is no separation between
nature and ourselves, we then start to heal
the world, for in healing the world, we heal
ourselves.
Spirit is always calling to you through Mother
Nature.
Take your time to listen to her speak, feel her
words through her soft green earth, listen to her
gentle breeze in your ear, open your eyes and see
all her beautiful signs in her flowers"
Mark Bajerski

THE PATHWAY TO HEALING

I'd like to say **THANK YOU** for coming this far on the journey with me. The stories we have walked through and experienced together shine a light on divine intervention and how it is here for each and every one of us. One only needs to clear the fears, the worries, the pressures of life and allow the love of Spirit to enter our hearts and lives. If you are asking the question, *"How can I learn to deepen the experience of divine intervention?"* then I come to you with some answers. The first is to understand one of our greatest challenges in this life; the battle between heart and mind!

Belief, knowing, love and truth...all things pure and good come from the heart. The heart is the gateway to spirituality and, through your awakening, your sense of Spirit will grow and you will find you live and work more from the heart. Ultimately, my message and hope is that one day, we can all achieve the goal of living and working from the heart where everything flows with love and peace.

The mind is, of course, essential to our everyday lives: what I refer to as the 'working mind' and focused thinking. That part of the mind which allows us to get on with our daily functions, for example: to look left and right before we cross the road; cross the 't's' and dot the 'i's'; to employ 'focused thinking' which helps us find solutions and achieve our goals. Be aware, however, of what I refer to as the 'thinking mind' the part which creates fear, worry, negativity...all things which keep us blocked and frozen. What I am hoping to give you are the tools needed to help you win your battle between heart and mind. By stilling the mind, our energy – our life force – is directed to where our body needs it the most. At this divine moment, we allow ourselves the joy of healing.

It is fair to say that most of us live in the mind. What I am asking of you today is to begin a life from the heart. Why is this necessary? Because by stilling the mind and living from the heart, we can achieve physical, emotional and long-lasting health and happiness. Some of you may be battling over the idea of how to still (silence) your mind and live from the heart – here is a quick and simple test to help you understand how powerful your mind is; how strong and just how long it will simply allow you to be happy, relaxed and self-heal.

Take a clock or watch and put it next to you. Gently close your eyes and try to clear all thoughts from your mind. Breathe and repeat this sentence: "This moment is MY moment. I do not have to worry or fear anything." Allow yourself to just 'be' in that moment. Focus on your breathing. You may experience 'mind chatter' coming through. For some of you, it may happen quickly and for others, it may take longer. Do your best to ignore the chatter and simply enjoy the stillness and peace around you. When you find that you have to open your eyes and continue with daily life, look at the watch. For how long did your mind allow you relax in that 'stillness'? Five minutes? Less? This simple test provides an indication of how long your mind can give you some 'time-out'. If you can only achieve five minutes or so, then can you now feel how your mind literally holds you captive from allowing much needed PEACE to flow into your life? If so, then now is a magical time of change!

Let the battle between the heart and mind begin. Good luck and remember, you are always worth the time.

Pure Energy Healing with the Elements: My Personal Secrets

I'm an ordinary man doing an extraordinary job. This has helped me to recognise all my faults as well as my gifts. Seeing ourselves in a true light gives us the opportunity to become better and stronger souls. With self-psychic healing we open up and discover what needs to be addressed inside the heart and mind.

When we embark on a journey to heal our mind, our body is healed at the same time. Our mind is rather like a filing cabinet where we store past issues; I describe this as 'unresolved paperwork.' When I look into clients' unanswered files I notice a dark, unhealthy energy which slowly seeps into their physical body. This is the route of many health issues. By regularly engaging in psychic healing I believe that illnesses and diseases can be cured or avoided altogether.

Today, you have been given a divine gift. By following the simple steps outlined in this chapter you'll understand that YOU, my dear friend, have the ability to heal yourself. Now is the time to begin your self-healing journey with me.

Please remember that my teachings do not involve any kind of pressures. There are no hard and fast rules about the "*When? Where? How?*" to carry out these exercises. Allow yourself to work these practices into your lifestyle in a way that suits you best. If you can find the time each day to carry out any one of the following steps, then that would be wonderful. However, if you don't get around to doing the exercises on any given day, then be happy; you didn't need to on that day!

Step I

Find a quiet place where you can still your thoughts. There's no set method to this; simply sit or lie down in a place where you feel comfortable. Breathe and relax for a few minutes with no sense of pressure. The exercise I'm about to share with you always works, so release any worries about whether it will or won't. Eliminate your fears and BELIEVE! This is a key component to healing. When you begin to feel more relaxed, your self-psychic healing has already started.

Step II

Your hands are the main instruments for self-healing, so concentrate on them. Focus on your bodily senses and you will begin to feel the energy flowing. Place your hands together for a few seconds then release them, until they're a few inches apart. Hold them there for a moment and feel how your body responds. You may feel pins and needles, heat or a repelling sensation. Do not rush this step. Slowly move your hands until they are about a foot apart then gently bring them together and apart again. Do this ten times and feel the energy. If you don't feel anything, there's no need to worry, though - feeling is not as important to self-healing as you may think.

Step III

Your left hand is your receiving hand, through which the universe delivers energy to you. Your right hand sends energy. Hold your left hand out and say these words out loud: "I ask for healing energy now and I accept any form of healing with gratitude." (In truth, it is not vital that you use the right hand for sending healing and the left hand to receive; use whichever one feels most comfortable and natural for you. Either way will work effectively.)

Step IV

Place your right hand about three to five inches above your stomach and move it in a circular motion clockwise. This is the point at which you may start to hear strange noises or have unusual sensations, feelings, or even pains in your body. Be open to anything new. This is what I call 'the heightened sense of healing.' I promise that if you relax and take your time you will feel something happening. The aim is to quieten your senses, open your heart and free your mind. When you have pinpointed an area which calls out to you, hover over it with your right hand. You will feel your hand growing warmer or, in some cases, colder. When the healing is complete you will be sent to another part of your body. This process may take five minutes, fifteen minutes or perhaps even longer, but remember – don't THINK, just FEEL. I self-heal every night and I no longer suffer from the irritable bowel syndrome which had haunted me for many years.

So now you know my simple secret to self-healing. All you need to remember is that practice makes perfect, as the saying goes. The exercise I have described is one which you can carry out in your home, your office – any quiet place where you can relax without interruption. The exercises which now follow are simple and effective ways in which we can receive healing through many natural elements provided by the universe and Mother Nature.

HEALING WITH THE ELEMENTS

Planet Earth is a most magnificent gift from the universe and Spirit. We have been given an abundance of resources which are all around us, and can help us to dispel the many negativities which are thrown at us on a daily basis. These negative forces can arise from the simplest of sources, such as conflicts with our loved one as we wake up that morning down to more serious matters such as natural disasters, wars and crime. Connecting to the elements provided to us by the universe is the most natural way to sustain our levels of positivity and sense of hopefulness, and to ensure we can bring love, hope and positive changes to our own lives and those of others.

There are three elements available to all of us on this beautiful planet, which can help to heal our negative baggage – the sea, the sun and trees (Nature). Soon, I will share with you some exercises which you can perform with these elements.

There are times when it is also important to 'cleanse' and clear away negative energy from our living and working spaces. I would like to share a most powerful and effective method with you now, using a natural herb – sage.

1. CLEANSING WITH SAGE

Clearing negative energy is so profound that I have made it my life's purpose. An effective method involves the burning of herbs, and the one I recommend above all others is sage. This wonderful herb has been used for thousands of years and it's amazing for cleansing your home, your business and any living space. Sage is grown all over the world but for this exercise, you need to use dried sage or sage sticks. You can find both on the internet or from a local herbal store or market – or, especially in the case of dried sage, even from your local supermarket.

First step, find yourself a suitable bowl – preferably wood, not metal, as the heat of the burning sage will penetrate and could burn your hands. A nice, thick, heavy wooden bowl is the best utensil to use when burning sage. When we say 'burning sage', this does not mean that we set the herb on fire! Our only intention is to release smoke which will cleanse the whole of the room or living space. Once the sage is set alight, immediately blow out the flame, reducing it to a burning cinder. The smoke released is what essentially cleanses the living space. Ensure the flame does not restart by blowing on the sage occasionally as you walk around the whole of the room or living space. Go from room to room, filling all the space with sage. The best way to do this is to walk around the room, going from wall to wall. Cleansing the walls will cleanse away the negative energy trapped from past and present. After thirty minutes, open all the windows to release this negative energy. You can safely dispose of the sage now.

2. THE DEEP BLUE SEA

The sea holds one of the most amazing healing gifts in the universe. All human beings are drawn to this vast body of water, which proves how powerful it is. I've been working with the sea to help heal people for some time now as it sucks away our worries and negative thoughts. That's why when you're near the sea, you can't explain it, but you feel lighter and happier. Each and every one of us can use the sea to heal ourselves.

Exercise to heal with the sea

If you have the opportunity to put your feet into the sea or, even better, to swim in it, you will feel its power - naturally cleansing and clearing away all the negative energy in and around your body. As stepping into the sea or taking a swim is not always possible, the following exercises will have the same effect, even if you are just sitting by the sea.

If possible, find yourself a nice, quiet place to sit where you feel very comfortable. The first stage is to create a connection to the sea. You can begin by simply taking in all its greatness - its depth;

its movement; its energy. Watch and listen as the waves move back and forth, creating wonderful reflections which sparkle along the water's surface. As you follow the flow and rhythm of the water, you will start to have feelings of calmness - letting go of all your daily worries and fears. Now, you will be living in the moment, and this is when you are ready to close your eyes.

The next stage is when we start to focus on our breathing. This is quite simple. We breathe in through the nose and breathe out through the mouth. Now, visualise yourself next to a vast healing bowl of water, ready to breathe in the healing energy through your nose. When you breathe out through your mouth, visualise all the negativity which is sitting inside you being released through with your breath. At the same time, as you breathe out, visualise all the negative aspects of your life: any physical or pains, or anything which disturbs or bothers you in any way - breathe them out! Remember, each time you breathe in through your nose, you are receiving the most powerful cleansing for your body. If you start to receive any beautiful sensations, messages or visualisations, then recognise that these are all messages for YOU from Spirit!

Many of us are not blessed to live close to the sea but don't worry! I have a great healing secret to share with you so you can bring the sea right into your home!

All you need is a large bowl, one bag of sea salt and some fresh water. Tip the whole bag of salt into the bowl and pour warm water on top (just hot enough so that the sea salt melts).

Place the bowl down onto the floor. Sit comfortably next to it. Remove your shoes and socks and place your feet in the bowl for thirty minutes. Alternatively, you can place this bowl on a bedside table or close to or under your bed. While you sleep, the salt water will act as a vacuum cleaner for your negative thoughts.

After you have completed the exercise, always remember to tip the bowl of sea water carefully down the toilet or sink. If any of the water touches your hands, wash them quickly for it now holds your negative energy.

This is an exercise which always brings results for my clients, my friends and also MYSELF. I have found it to be one of the most beneficial ways to keep the mind free from stress.

3. THE SUN

We all have access to the sun, but in certain countries it's not so usual to see it every day. Nevertheless, when it does come out to play, go outside and bask in it, for the sun's energy will help to heal you. We are all made very aware how the sun heals us physically by providing us with the essential vitamin D. Just as you do with the sea, you need to open yourself to the healing energy and splendour of the sun - opening your arms and asking the sun for its healing power. Throughout history and across all religions, the sun has always been symbolised as a life force of this universe. Quite simply, it is your feelings which will allow the sun to heal you. The sun is right in front of our eyes, yet few people realise or fully understand its healing powers. I'm not asking you to worship the sun – just somewhere in between! And please do be sensible; it is never wise to carry out the following exercises when the sun is at its hottest. I recommend very early morning or late afternoon for sun-healing (and not sun-burning!)

Exercise to heal with the sun

Sit facing the sun but do not look directly into it, as this will harm your eyes. When you're sitting comfortably, relax for a few minutes. Inhale through your nose and count to five as you breathe in the sun's energy. Stop and hold your breath for another five seconds. Then release by exhaling out through your mouth, counting out five seconds again. Hold your breath for a further five seconds. Repeat this breathing exercise until you feel lighter. Begin to feel the sun coming closer to you. Imagine a powerful energy flowing directly from the sun into your heart. Allow that energy to spread throughout the whole of your body. As you continue to do this, you will find yourself at the point which I call 'ultimate energy'. This is a powerful and positive energy. At times, you may hold onto it and at other times, you can decide to send it back out to the world. Either way it is all perfect as when you carry this energy with you, it will always have a great effect on those around you.

Exercise to Send Healing to Others

This ultimate energy deserves ultimate healing thoughts. Anyone who comes to mind - family, loved ones, pets, anyone who may be going through a difficult and challenging time and indeed, anyone who may present a challenge to YOU - are all deserving of pure energy healing. My simple secret to sending this energy is to just see them HAPPY; see them WELL; see them HEALED! Anyone suffering from a physical, mental or emotional issue – visualise that person or animal as already healed. This is the focus of true healing and in your moment of healing or sending healing, no issues exist.

Thousands of years ago, many civilisations worshipped the sun because of its healing qualities. This knowledge had been lost and forgotten – but not any longer!

4. TREES (NATURE)

Last but not least, let's take a look at the wonders of trees. I've shared my own personal and divine experience earlier in this book – I have found MY TREE. Without question, I feel the power of cleansing and clearing of all my negative energy from this, my beautiful tree, on a daily basis.

Trees balance the universe – when you find yourself next to a tree, you will find yourself 'in balance.' We need to recognise how important Mother Nature is, and how we are killing both her and ourselves. The air we breathe comes from the trees around us – how much more divine or important can that be in our lives and those of our children?

Perhaps today you can make a pledge to Mother Nature: don't cut down trees – go and plant one! Plant your very own tree and feel the reward that Mother Nature will give you.

Exercise to Heal with a Tree

Find a park or wooded area which is safe, familiar and comfortable to you. Walk around it and take in the trees about you. Take your time – when you find yourself drawn to a particular tree, sit next to it. Allow yourself to connect to the amazing strength of the tree; feel the peace surrounding you. Visit your tree a few times to become connected with its energy and before long, you will start to experience deeper feelings about yourself and your life. These are the 'connecting moments.' They don't happen every time you're near your tree, so never force your feelings as they should just flow.

A day will arrive when you feel you know your tree; you will recognise a connection. At this stage, find a place to sit comfortably and close your eyes. Inhale through your nose and count to three as you breathe in the tree's energy. Stop and hold your breath for a further three seconds. Now exhale out of your mouth, counting to three again. Hold your breath for a further three seconds. Repeat this breathing exercise until you feel lighter. You will soon feel an inner strength through the *clearing and cleansing of the tree's energy.*

This energy clears all negativity, all thoughts, fears and worries. Now is the moment we need to 'let go'. Allow all of this energy to flow through your feet and hands. Give the tree your negative energy

– feel this energy flow through your feet into the roots, out through your hands and onto the bark of the tree. If you are facing challenging moments in your life, ask your tree for help and wisdom to conquer these challenges. This is something I do myself on a regular basis with extremely positive outcomes. As a suggestion, say the following words to your tree in exchange for this clearing and support: "Today I make a promise to be truthful and honest to my fellow friend, to be the best energy I can be, and to help heal the world from my heart." Then carry out this agreement in a way that is most suited to your daily lifestyle. Get ready for a new energy of abundance to flow through your daily life and enhanced happiness and health, like never before. Trees heal body, mind and soul.

5. SURRENDERING!

When the self-healing exercises I have mentioned become part of your daily living, be aware that you'll sometimes come up against blocks. This is a test to see if you're strong enough to rise above the challenge. Once you recognise that you want to change your life, then your journey on this magical path will have begun. It's at this point that you need to surrender to the universe, which is easier than you may think.

Exercise
For one week, make a commitment and say, "This week I will not worry and I will not focus on

the coming seven days. I will live in the moment and I will trust that everything will be divinely laid out for me." As you repeat these words, know that a healing process has already begun, and it is helping you along your path. You'll feel these words resonating in and around your energy.

This is called pure energy healing; it is all love and no ego. If you work on this principle and the self-healing methods in this chapter, I promise that the universe will stop and take notice of you. No matter how tough life can be at times, you must remember that the universe has nothing against you personally. It's one of the most important lessons we all need to learn here on earth. Being aware of challenges and blocks is not enough: we must learn to conquer these lessons.

When I started on my path, I practised this every day. Now, I have no need to 'surrender'. I already live in the moment. I have deleted my past and I leave my future to the universe. Start saying this today and this week; take a holiday from your mind and see what happens.

YOU CAN DO IT!
I believe in you and I know who you are.
You are a beautiful soul.
You are my brother.
You are my sister.
You are part of me.
Together we can heal ourselves
Together we can heal the world.

AWAKENING – STEPS TO SPIRITUAL AWARENESS

1. You are becoming more in-tune and connected to Spirit when . . .
2. You start to feel happy and don't know why.
3. You become more aware of people's sadness and start to feel the urge to help.
4. You become less interested in conflicts.
5. You start to wear an uncontrollable smile on your face.
6. You start to have an uncontrollable desire of peace and stillness.
7. You start to find yourself going out into Nature.
8. You start to believe and trust in everything.
9. You find yourself not thinking at all.
10. You start to see the positive in the negative.
11. You spend time looking at yourself and asking whether your actions affected anyone in a negative or positive way.
12. You don't take anything to heart and you start to see others in a new light.
13. You become more and more forgiving.
14. You start to use the words love, happiness and energy more each day.
15. You don't waste your energy trying to make people understand your beliefs.
16. Your friends start to say there is something different about you, but they don't know what.
17. You start to buy wooden signs from shops reciting wise words and quotes.

18. You start to give gifts to your friends and family.
19. You start to write a book about your life.
20. You begin to feel less frustration, worry and anger towards others and yourself.
21. You start to ask yourself who you are and why you are here.
22. You find yourself becoming more patient.
23. You are not so bothered about drinking alcohol.
24. You don't seem to need to eat as much.
25. You find yourself not analysing every situation.

The Journey Continues

At this very moment, I live on a mountain in the south of Spain. My coming here was no accident: I know now it was purely and simply down to synchronicity. The mountain which has become my home is truly magical; of that I am sure. Since my arrival here eight years ago, my life has been transformed. This transformation happened through those whom I have met, those who have been brought to me and through all the experiences we have shared together. I have faced and overcome many challenges during these years.

The journey to the completion of this book - my very first - has been thoroughly enjoyable, though it was also not without certain challenges. What is important in facing our challenges is to take courage and when it is needed, not to be afraid to ask for help. We are all brothers and sisters; we are all here to learn; we are all here to help one another. Allow others to give to you freely. Don't say no to a helping hand when offered in friendship; smile and receive from your heart. In allowing others to help you, they receive the opportunity to learn a valuable lesson – the gift of learning HOW to give freely).

My pure intention for this book is to relight the flame of Spirit and raise the level of awareness of our 'one-ness.'

SPIRIT EXISTS IN OUR WORLD and by accepting Spirit into our lives, we are open to a happier and more peaceful existence – we are always loved and supported. The changes in my life over the past eight years are testament to this fact, along with the beautiful accounts of Spirit's work in the lives of others that I have shared with you in this book.

What's next is up to you...so...make a start today!

Look back through the pages of this book and share any words and ideas that really resonate with you. Create your own personal affirmations from the words from Spirit and place them around your home, email them to your loved ones or post them on Facebook. I am happy for you to share these words as it is Spirit's intention that we all share with and help one another as we work toward raising the vibration of this world.

As you find the above steps starting to resonate with you, all I want to say is: congratulations. You are becoming more spiritually enlightened and closer to the top of your own personal mountain!

My sincere hope is that this little book may have helped you in a beautiful way along this path to enlightenment. If you would like to share the joy I hope this book has added to your life, perhaps think of someone you feel may be helped in some way from reading it. Then, wrap it up with love and gift it to them freely. One of the greatest lessons I have learned through Spirit is one of my most important daily practices, and it seems fitting to leave you today with this powerful thought. I hope it may become a daily practice for you too.

'The Heart that gives is always full.'
With all my love, Mark Bajerski

"Once we are blessed with healing, when we are open to receiving a new energy, one that the universe gives so freely;
There is nothing that can stop your light from spreading around the world for others to see and to feel. Never limit yourself by a belief that you have no power.
Every single one of us has an inner Light - embrace this gift and allow your Light to shine"
Mark Bajerski

KIND WORDS

'*Mark, truly inspirational!*'
Kerry Katona; British singer and media personality.

'*Mark doesn't impose his own personality. He focuses on the connection to your energy, with impressive results.*'
Mark Curry; television presenter.

'*There is an almost desperate need for positivity in the world and Mark gives clarity to anyone who is seeking both strength and courage, allowing you to get in touch with your own positivity. This man works magic.*'
Sarah Tucker; author, journalist and TV presenter.

'*Mark just reached the level to be able to communicate things to me that totally amazed me ... I did not think too much about the 'how?' I was most comfortable with knowing that it felt genuine and real and just left me feeling so much at ease, comfortable, happy and excited.*'
Andy McGrath; EA to Director of Television, ITV, London

'*Seeing Mark helped erode anxiety in my life and with greater confidence, I can enjoy life more; afterwards it's like you're driving through life in an open top car on a sunny, summer day.*'
Christian Gardner; former UN Ambassador, Southern Spain

Ranked Spain's No 1 by 'America's & World's Best Psychics & Healers Who Care Most About You 2012/13.

91049278R00092

Made in the USA
Middletown, DE
28 September 2018